ALSO BY CAROL BURNETT

This Time Together

One More Time

CAROL BURNETT

Carrie and Me

A Mother-Daughter Love Story

Simon & Schuster

New York   London   Toronto   Sydney   New Delhi

Simon & Schuster
1230 Avenue of the Americas
New York, NY 10020

First Simon & Schuster hardcover edition April 2013

SIMON & SCHUSTER and colophon are registered trademarks
of Simon & Schuster, Inc.

For information about special discounts for bulk purchases,
please contact Simon & Schuster Special Sales at
1-866-506-1949 or business@simonandschuster.com.

The Simon & Schuster Speakers Bureau can bring authors
to your live event. For more information or to book an event,
contact the Simon & Schuster Speakers Bureau at
1 866 248 3049 or visit our website at www.simonspeakers.com.

Designed by Ruth Lee-Mui

Manufactured in the United States of America

1   3   5   7   9   10   8   6   4   2

Library of Congress Cataloging-in-Publication Data
Burnett, Carol.
Carrie and me : a mother-daughter love story / Carol Burnett.
1st Simon & Schuster hardcover ed.
p. cm.
1. Burnett, Carol. 2. Burnett, Carol—Family. 3. Entertainers—United States—Biography.
4. Comedians—United States—Biography. 5. Mothers and daughters—United States—
Biography. 6. Hamilton, Carrie. 7. Actors—United States—Biography.
8. Television writers—United States—Biography. I. Title.
PN2287.B85A3 2013
792.702'8092—dc23
[B]
2012033095
ISBN 978-1-4767-0641-2
ISBN 978-1-4767-0642-9 (ebook)

Photo credits can be found on page 203.

For Jody and Erin

Carrie and Me

PREFACE

In late 2000, my daughter Carrie Hamilton was working on a story, "Sunrise in Memphis," writing in her small Colorado cabin. The story was about a bohemian girl's strange road trip to Elvis's Graceland with a mysterious cowboy. Carrie planned to turn it into a screenplay eventually. Because she felt a kinship with Kate, her main character, Carrie (being a free spirit and somewhat bohemian herself) decided to hit the road and take the same trip for research purposes.

So she got out her maps, filled the gas tank in her Jeep, and headed south toward Memphis. She e-mailed me fresh pages of the story almost daily, along with tales of her own adventures on her journey to Graceland. As a side trip, Carrie visited our family's old stomping grounds in San Antonio, Texas, and Belleville, Arkansas, since the two of us were writing a play together based on my family, who came from those parts of the country.

Carrie didn't live to finish either project. She died of cancer a little over a year later at the age of thirty-eight.

This book has taken me on a bittersweet journey. When she was in the hospital for the last time, Carrie asked me to finish "Sunrise in Memphis" for her, which I haven't been able to do. Try as I might, the characters in the story were hers to write, not mine. Carrie's request had been living with me for over ten years when I finally figured out what I *could* do.

Fortunately, I had saved all of the letters and e-mails we wrote to each other during her road trip to Memphis. In Part One of this book I've combined that correspondence with my own memories. These include a few episodes I've written about before, but I feel they bear repeating to round out the order of events. I've also written here about Carrie's brave fight against her illness. Part Two is Carrie's story "Sunrise in Memphis," which is fun to read in its own right, but also eerily echoes Carrie's journey.

This book is my way of honoring her last request, bringing to the page many of Carrie's thoughts and feelings and also my own journey with her, including all the ups and downs in the early years (which got pretty bumpy when Carrie became a teenager).

Carrie was widely known as a magnetic young woman with a stunning smile, an infectious laugh, a throaty voice, and the soul of a poet. She was someone who cared deeply for others, particularly for those less fortunate. Whenever a homeless person approached her, she would offer them a deal: five dollars if they told her their story. As you'll see, Carrie used those stories, and the personal narratives shared with her by everyone she met, as inspiration for her prose, her poetry, her music, her lyrics, and her acting. Carrie piled so much into her young life that one can only imagine what she would have tackled and accomplished in the second half.

For myself, I hope you will get to know the daughter I loved and cherished. I can honestly say that just about everyone who knew Carrie loved her. Maybe that's because she loved them right back.

I also hope I've succeeded in bringing Carrie's essence to these pages. I treasure her words, and even after reading them again and again, each time I am grateful for the reminder that she has never left me.

PART ONE

Carrie and Me

Some Very Early Memories

December 1963
New York City

In spite of the cold, snowy weather, I was very hot all the time because I was very pregnant. One night I was burning up, but didn't dare open the window in our apartment bedroom for fear that my husband, Joe Hamilton, sleeping next to me, might wind up freezing to death. So I went into the second bedroom, opened the window to let the cold night air blow in, and plopped myself down on top of the covers. At last I was finally comfortable. The next morning I woke up refreshed after a good night's sleep and found myself covered in a lovely white blanket of snow, which had blown in sideways through the open window during the night! Heaven.

I went into labor the evening of December 4. Small pains at first, but we knew this was it. Joe and I checked into the hospital around eight o'clock, and I was assigned to a labor room. The night nurse, Louise (I remember her name because it was my mother's name), helped me get undressed and issued me the regular hospital uniform—a singularly unattractive, knee-length gown, opening in the back. She hung up my dress and coat in the closet, put my boots on the shelf, and led me to a rather lumpy bed. I obediently got in and she hoisted up some metal bars on both sides. I figured she must be worried that I might roll off onto the floor and bounce down the hall.

A doctor on duty came in to examine me, and my water broke immediately.

A short while later, Joe was ushered in and was advised by Louise that he might as well go home because it looked like it would be a long night. I secretly wished he would stay with me, but in those days the father wasn't necessarily a welcome figure in the labor room. Louise promised Joe she'd call him when the time drew near. They left, and I was alone in the dark. The nurse had given me a shot and I dozed off, thinking this labor thing wasn't nearly as difficult as they say. . . .

The next thing I remember is waking to the sound of some woman from the cell next to mine screaming, "Omigod! Omigod! Get this out of me NOW!!!" I dozed off again, still confident that *my* labor was going to be a snap.

Wrong. I was awakened by pains coming fast and hard. I called out for Louise. She came in, gave me a few ice chips to chew on, assured me that all was well, and left me once again. All was well, my foot! I thought the shot they had given me earlier was going to make this whole business easier. It only made me drunk. So drunk that I sat up, pushed the bed bars down, got up, waddled over to the closet, and proceeded to get dressed. I had put on my dress and coat, and was trying to squeeze into my boots when Louise came back in.

"Mrs. Hamilton! What are you doing?"

"Leaving."

"But you can't!"

"Look," I reasoned, "I didn't feel like this when I came in, so I won't feel like this when I get out of here!"

She got me back into that god-awful gown and into that god-awful bed, and the whole thing started back up with a vengeance. Before long I found myself sounding just like my next-door neighbor.

Carrie Louise Hamilton, my firstborn child, arrived the morning of December 5 at 11:20 a.m. They placed her in my arms and when I looked at my little miracle, all that pain quickly became a dim memory.

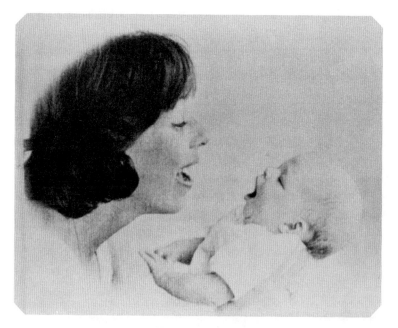

Holding my new baby daughter, Carrie Louise, 1963

I remember wanting Carrie to walk by her first birthday. She had already taken the first few baby steps by the time she was eleven months old, but only when we walked together, so she could hold on to my little finger. I came up with a brilliant idea. I would hold on to one end of a large handkerchief and give Carrie the other end (which substituted for my little finger). It worked. Together we walked up and down the hall of our apartment several times a day for about a week, and she never fell down. Then came the day when I quietly dropped my end of the handkerchief, but continued to walk beside her. Not noticing, she walked without my help to the end of the hall. I was so excited I exclaimed, "Good girl!!! See? You did it all by yourself!" She looked at the handkerchief, and seeing that I wasn't holding the other end, immediately plopped down on the floor and started to cry. After that I let her learn to walk at her own pace, having come to the realization that there are some things a parent shouldn't try to force.

In 1966, Joe and I relocated to Los Angeles, where we eventually welcomed two more little girls into our family, Jody and Erin. Our variety show premiered in the fall of 1967 when Jody was eight months old, and Erin was born in August of 1968 during our summer hiatus. So now we had three beautiful little girls.

Carrie, Joe holding Jody, and I'm holding baby Erin

We bought Betty Grable's old house. She had been one of my favorite movie stars when I was growing up, so it was a particular thrill to know that she had walked (or tap-danced!) in those very halls. It was a sheer delight for me when, in the very first season of *The Carol Burnett Show,* Betty Grable was a guest!

As our family settled into life in California, Joe and I made sure our work schedules gave us plenty of time to be with the girls. Usually I went to work after the girls had gone off to school and I would often be out in time to pick them up. Dinner was at six o'clock every night. The only time we worked all day was during our Friday tapings. When the girls were old enough, they would attend our early dress rehearsal and wind up having their pictures taken with our guests each week. Our show would take two weeks off at Christmas, one week off for Easter vacation, and the entire summer off! It was a perfect schedule for parents of three small children.

Jody, Erin, and Carrie: three peas in a pod

When Carrie was about five I thought it would be a swell idea to send her to ballet school. Outfitted in her tights and a leotard, she happily leaped around with the other little girls. One afternoon I was driving her home from a class, and she started to cry. "What's the matter, sweetie?"

"I have to pee-pee!!!!"

I drove as fast as I could and pulled into our driveway several minutes later. We jumped out of the car and sprinted into the house. Too late. She had let loose with the waterworks and her leotard and tights were completely soaked. She was bawling her eyes out over the humiliation of it all, and declared in no uncertain terms that she didn't want to continue with the lessons anymore because "IT'S NOT EASY BEING A BALLE-RINA!"

Needless to say, this time (having learned my lesson from the handkerchief-walking episode) I didn't try to force her to continue. . . .

Not too long afterward, it was time for Carrie to enter kindergarten. We had enrolled her in a small school not far from where we lived and when the big day came Carrie was excited as all get-out. "I'm a big girl now!!!"

The principal, Mrs. Vickers, had told me to pull my car up to the curb in front of the school, where she would meet us at nine a.m. I figured I would go with Carrie into her classroom, get her settled in, and then leave after a few minutes.

When we pulled up to the curb, Mrs. Vickers was there, waiting for us. All of a sudden I noticed several cars waiting in line behind me: other mothers were dropping off their kids, too. I stopped, and Mrs. Vickers opened Carrie's door and proceeded to take Carrie by the hand and slam the door, yelling to me: "PULL AWAY! PULL AWAY!" At that moment, it dawned on me that I would not be walking my daughter into her classroom on her first day of school.

Startled, Carrie began to cry and Mrs. Vickers picked her up in her arms, telling me once again to "PULL AWAY!" As I peeled out, I saw the other cars dropping off their little passengers, and also "pulling away." Looking in the rearview mirror, I saw my baby crying for me as I rounded the corner. I was as miserable as she was.

I drove home and sat staring at the clock ticking away the l-o-n-g minutes until I could pick Carrie up at noon. "Surely, she must've been okay once she got into class and met all the other kids," I prayed. After three hours, which seemed like three years, noon finally arrived and I tore out of the house. This time I parked down the block and walked up to the school, so I could speak with Mrs. Vickers (without having to "pull away") and ask her how Carrie had done.

"She sat alone on the play yard bench the whole three hours, but I'm sure she'll warm up in time." (*Oh great!*) I found Carrie still sitting on the bench in the play yard. She rushed up to me and threw her arms around my legs. Both of us were crying.

Back in the car on the way home, she looked up at me and smiled, "Boy, Mommy, am I glad THAT'S over with!"

At that moment, I didn't have the heart to tell her that school lasts more than just one day. We stopped for an ice cream cone before I broke the news to her.

Carrie, still not too thrilled about kindergarten

One day we caught Carrie in a fib. I don't even remember what it was exactly, but Joe and I felt it was important to send her upstairs to her room and to bed right after dinner. It couldn't have been much of a lie. She was only six, but we wanted to make sure it registered with her that fibbing was not a good thing.

After a few minutes I knocked on the door and entered the bedroom she shared with her sister Jody. We were alone. Carrie was in her PJs and under the covers. She had been crying. I sat on the edge of the bed and kissed her, wiping the tears away.

"Sweetheart. Your daddy and I love you very much. You know that, don't you?"

"Uh-huh . . ."

"We love you, but we don't like what you did. Do you understand the difference?"

She nodded. I moved closer. "Honey, you can always tell us

the truth, no matter what, and we'll still love you. That will never change."

She was staring at me. Hard. I moved even closer. Face-to-face.

"It's just that telling fibs or lies can only lead to bigger fibs and bigger lies and then things get worse and worse. And we don't want that, now, do we?"

Carrie hadn't blinked or taken her eyes off me. I was really getting through to her. By this time, we were just about nose to nose. I seized the opportunity to expand on the importance of honest communication, moving on to talk about how love could overcome any differences we might ever have, etc., etc. "Never be afraid to come and talk to us about anything. I promise Daddy and I will listen, and we will work it out, no matter what it is."

She was looking at me, mesmerized. This had been going on for several minutes and she was still drinking in what I was saying with all her heart! I was so proud of myself, and of how I was handling the situation that, I swear, in the back of my mind, I heard violins. Somebody, somewhere, was about to present me with a medal for "Mother of the Year."

I finally finished, and asked Carrie if she had anything to ask me.

"Uh-huh."

"What, darling? Anything. Just ask."

"How many teeth do you have?"

Taking three little girls, ages three to seven, out to dinner proved to be a challenge, to say the least. We'd dress them in their jeans and sweatshirts, pile them into the car, and head for Carmine's, the local Italian restaurant. Joe and I barely made it through some meals with our sanity intact, and several times it just plain didn't work. The difficulty was that on any given evening, one, two, or all three of the girls would turn out to be a handful. They would argue with one another, or not want to eat what they had ordered, or (on occasion) open their mouths flashing unswallowed food to crack one another up, or fall asleep at the table in spite of the early hour. So Joe and I gave up trying for several weeks.

Then one day I got an idea. I put on a makeup smock that I had in my closet, and taped a sign on my bedroom door: BEAUTY SALON. PLEASE KNOCK FOR AN APPOINTMENT. THE COST OF A BRAND-NEW HAIRDO IS ONE PENNY.

In a few short minutes, I heard a knock and when I opened the door, there stood Carrie (who could read the sign) with Jody and Erin in line behind her. Each one had a penny in her hand. Carrie, being the oldest, opted to go first.

I said, "Yes, madam? May I be of service?"

Catching on, Carrie replied, "I would like to get a new hairdo."

"Right this way, madam." I led her into my bathroom and sat her down in front of the mirror at my dressing table. "Would madam like a pageboy or a flip?"

Unsure, she simply stared into the mirror.

I ran my fingers through her hair and looking at her through the mirror, I said, "Madam, with your lovely features, may I suggest a pageboy?"

She nodded, and I proceeded to wash and towel-dry her hair. I might add that this was the easiest time I ever had washing her hair. No complaints about soap in her eyes, etc., etc. She became the ideal client.

We returned to the mirror, and I began to blow-dry her hair

with a brush, and then applied a curling iron to turn her hair under. When I was finished, she was sporting a perfect pageboy.

"Now, madam, why don't you pick out a nice dress to wear out to dinner tonight?" I held out my hand for the penny, which she happily shelled out before she ran to her room to pick out a DRESS!

Jody was next, and the whole scenario played out again, with Jody opting for a flip. Then she, too, headed for her closet and chose a nice blue dress.

Erin was next, wanting a pageboy like Carrie's. I helped her pick out a pink dress.

Joe and I waited for them to come downstairs, dressed and ready to go. They waltzed into the living room, all three pleased as punch with their new "looks."

All through dinner they acted like perfect little ladies.

Joe asked me later, "How did you know this would work?"

"Simple. We all act differently depending on what we're wearing and how we look. The girls felt grown-up, so they acted like it."

I've always believed that kids are great actors. They "become" what they look like. Halloween is a good example. As pirates, they "swashbuckle" with the best of them. As cowboys, they swagger, bowlegged, with their hands on their holsters, and tip their hats *just so*. As witches, they can cackle like Margaret Hamilton in *The Wizard of Oz*. As princesses, they can dance and twirl like Cinderella, and as fairies they seem to *glide* . . .

I remember a time when I was in the company of the brilliant English actor Laurence Olivier, and he was talking about how he gets into character. "I'm never quite sure how I'm going to act a role until I figure out what 'HE'S' going to look like. I'm particularly fond of 'remodeling' my nose! Sometimes it can sport a bump, or sometimes I'll make the nostrils wider . . . it's lots of fun to hide yourself behind makeup or a certain costume."

I couldn't agree more. During my variety show, I often didn't know how I was going to perform a sketch until I had a powwow with our multitalented costume designer, Bob Mackie. For instance, when Tim Conway created the characters of Mr. Tudball and Mrs. Wiggins, my character of the ditzy secretary ("whom the IQ Fairy never visited") was originally written to be a dotty senior citizen. When I went to the costume fitting that week, Bob showed me a sketch he had drawn of an altogether different Mrs. Wiggins. She was a blond bimbo wearing a flowery blouse with a push-up bra, and a tight black skirt, plus stilettos. When I tried on the skirt, we found it sagged in the rear end. I said to Bob, "I think we'll have to take it in, because I'm pretty flat in the behind."

"No we won't. Just stick your butt out where it's sagging."

That's exactly what I did, and, as a result, I wound up with a most peculiar shape, because of my posture, plus an odd "waddle walk" because of the tight skirt and the stilettos, which eventually became the character's trademark. All these crazy choices opened up the character of Mrs. Wiggins for me. In other words, now I knew who she was, and how to portray her—simply because of how she looked and how she walked!

So that's how I came up with the "game" for the girls and their hairdos.

I was pretty pleased with myself. Not only did the game work, but I was three pennies richer! (And I still have them to this day.)

All through grammar school, Carrie excelled in her classes, never bringing home any grades lower than a B-plus, but more often As. She won the school's coveted Silver Bowl when she was graduating from the sixth grade for not only having the best grades, but also for being the most popular student. I almost exploded with pride when her name was announced.

By the time Carrie entered the seventh grade in junior high, she had sprouted up and become noticeably taller than her classmates. She was reed thin (best described as gangly), and I knew she worried about her big feet, the railroad-track braces on her teeth, and her stringy ash-blond hair. Still the question caught me by surprise.

"Mama, am I ugly?"

"Why would you think that, sweetheart?"

"Because I am. I'm ugly."

"Well, you're not. You're just going through that awkward age, that's all. Before you know it, you'll turn into a butterfly!"

"I'll never be a butterfly."

"Of course you will."

"No I won't!"

That should have been a red flag for me, but I truly believed what I said to myself: "It's simply a stage she's going through, that's all."

In 1978, I had decided that we should end our eleven-year run of *The Carol Burnett Show*. Even though CBS wanted us back for a twelfth season, I felt it was time to move on. I wanted to be able to pick and choose projects that would give me even more time to spend at home. Also, I believed it was better to leave before someone from the network would eventually knock on our door and say, "Stop doing this!" Our final taping was in March of that year. It was a bittersweet ending, but I felt it was the right thing to do.

Even though I was home much more, Carrie was becoming more and more agitated. As much as I tried to get her off her pity-pot, she kept digging in her heels, and over the next year, in spite of the fact that her braces had come off and many of her friends were now as tall as she was, Carrie seemed to be losing all the self-esteem she had enjoyed in grammar school.

Diary entry:

> I wish I could get through to her, but damn it, she cuts me off at the pass every single time. Whenever I want to have a talk with her, to communicate, she either ignores me or says she's tired and retires to her room. Also, she seems to be losing her appetite. Is this all about puberty? I know being a teenager is a pain in the ass, but her attitude is becoming a pain in _my_ ass, too!
>
> TEENAGERS!
>
> Quite frankly, there are times I'd like to sedate her and wake her up when she's twenty.

In my naïveté I continued to "know" that she would grow out of it. But Carrie didn't know it, or believe it, and I later learned that she began to "experiment" to make her feel better about herself. She had always aimed to be the best at anything she tried, and it didn't take long for Carrie to become the best drug addict in her group at high school. However, Joe and I were still in the dark about what she was doing. She was fourteen.

Diary entry:

> *Now I'm really getting worried. Carrie brought home her*
> *report card and it was filled with Ds and a couple of Cs. It's not*
> *like her. She doesn't talk much at home anymore, either. She*
> *and Jody and Erin used to chatter like magpies at the dinner*
> *table. Now it's just Erin and Jody. Joe asked her what was wrong*
> *tonight, and she said, "I have a headache." He shot back, "Seems*
> *like you've had a headache an awful lot lately." She excused*
> *herself, took her half empty plate into the kitchen, and went up*
> *to her room without so much as a goodnight.*

As parents, Joe and I were unbelievably naïve about the whole
situation, in spite of the fact that Joe had been in recovery for several years, and both my parents had died of alcoholism. I was in a
state of denial, convinced that all the "bad stuff" I'd gone through
in my younger years was a thing of the past. It wasn't until Carrie's grades went from As to Fs that we started to suspect it was
due to more than mere growing pains.

Diary entry:

> *Joe and I had a long talk with Carrie after she got home*
> *from school today. There were big circles under her eyes. We asked*
> *her if she was on any drugs. She said no and started to cry. We*
> *talked to her at length about the dangers of using drugs. She*
> *calmed down and nodded at everything we were saying. I want*
> *to believe her. Dear God, I want to believe her!*

Over the next few weekends we encouraged Carrie to have some of her girlfriends come over and spend time at our house. They did, but they would just hole up in her room for the afternoon. Things didn't improve. Carrie was still hidden and distant. I was afraid of who she was becoming. One morning I made the tough decision to search her room. At first I felt guilty, but my fear over-rode my conscience and, after she left for school, I went into her bedroom and started to poke around. . . .

Diary entry:

>   *Dear God in heaven! I found some marijuana hidden in one of Carrie's shoes in her closet. When Joe got home, I showed it to him and he was fit to be tied. I cried all day. My worst nightmare has come true.*
>
>   *When Carrie got home we showed her what we'd found and she got furious with me for being a "snoop." She screamed at both of us, burst into tears, and ran into her room. Oh God, I'm heartsick. What have we done? What did we do wrong? Why is this happening?? What can we do to help her?? I feel so helpless. . . .*

We grounded Carrie, but allowed her to have her girlfriends over, making sure they checked their purses downstairs on the kitchen counter before they went up to her room, in case they were bringing drugs. (As if that would do any good. They could've hidden them anywhere in their clothes. *How stupid were we?*)

Carrie would sleep away the weekends behind her closed bedroom door, coming down to the kitchen to grab something to eat, and then retreating back into her room. Joe and I both figured she was getting drugs at school. But how? She didn't have any money. Then, while he was getting dressed one morning Joe discovered one of his watches was missing. He stormed out of our bedroom, and the next thing I knew he was taking Carrie's door off the hinges! (As if *that* would do any good.)

Nothing worked.

I would go into Carrie's room late at night to make sure she was breathing. Several times, when she was very still, I would put a mirror under her nose. When I saw the fog, I would think to myself, "Thank God, she's okay." I would sit on her bed and cry for hours. I remember wailing to Joe, "I'm at my wits' end, what can we do?"

The whole family was in an upheaval. Jody and Erin were torn between being loyal to Carrie by keeping whatever secrets they knew, and worrying themselves sick over their beloved big sister. One of the secrets was that after everyone had gone to sleep, Jody, who at this time was around eleven, would sometimes help Carrie sneak out of the house late at night by turning off the alarm, allowing Carrie time to make her exit, and then turn it back on. Jody would then sit up for an hour or so, waiting for Carrie to call her to tell her she was on her way home. Then Jody would disarm the security system again, turning it back on when Carrie was safely inside the house. When Jody confessed this to me much later I asked why she would do such a thing. "Because I didn't want her to get in trouble with you and Dad. I wanted to help my big sister."

Meanwhile, Carrie was losing weight, staying home from school, and becoming more and more sullen. This went on for more than a year. We were terrified that she could be killing herself.

Diary entry:

I'm positive it's not just pot anymore. Something tells me she has graduated to heavier drugs. I find myself treading on eggshells around her all the time now. I'm scared to upset her because it might trigger more use, and I'm scared if I'm not strict enough she'll sink even lower. Scared if I DO, scared if I DON'T. I'm just one big ball of fear.

Joe and I decided to see a psychologist who specialized in substance abuse. We had lost all confidence in our ability to handle Carrie. Nothing we said or did helped. The doctor explained that this was a "family disease" and should be treated as such. He recommended a rehab facility in Houston, Texas, the Palmer Drug Abuse Program (PDAP), which specialized in teenaged drug abuse.

Diary entry:

We flew to Houston today and admitted Carrie into the rehab hospital, where they tell us she will be weaned from whatever it is she's been taking. She'll be there for thirty days, going to meetings, and having one-on-one sessions with counselors who themselves are recovering addicts. The head counselor told us, "It's like when kids get braces on their teeth, they don't want to hear from their parents or the dentist, they want to get the scoop from another kid who has gone through the same thing." He said that at the end of the thirty days the family would be invited to come and attend family groups for a week.

When it came time to say good-bye Carrie wouldn't look at

us. She was so angry with Joe and me for putting her in rehab
that she wore a T-shirt with SING-SING *written on the front.*

Carrie was just fifteen. That evening, in spite of the day we had
gone through, I actually slept through the night, knowing that for
the time being she was safe in a lockdown situation. I was so tired
of worrying and crying. Jody and Erin were upset with Joe and
me. They didn't want Carrie to be "sent away." We explained to
them that we'd all fly to Houston in a month for "Family Week,"
and bring Carrie back home with us.

We weren't allowed to speak to Carrie for the first two weeks
and the days dragged by. When we finally could call, she spoke to
me, Joe, and her sisters, wanting to know if we all would come
for "Family Week" at the end of her thirty-day stay. Before we
hung up she said, "I love you, Mama." My heart almost exploded
with happiness.

Diary entry:

> *"Family Week" was amazing! When we got to the PDAP*
> *headquarters, Carrie was waiting on the steps. When she saw Joe,*
> *me, and her sisters, she ran up to us, crying, and threw her arms*
> *around all four of us. Jody and Erin were already crying, and Joe*
> *and I joined in. She's not mad at us anymore! She introduced us*
> *to other patients and to her counselors. She looks wonderful. She*
> *has gained some weight and has color in her cheeks!!! Omigod,*
> *I'm so grateful. Thank you, God. Thank you! Thank you!*

Joe, Jody, Erin, Carrie, and I attended the twelve-step meetings
at PDAP together, and Carrie got up and shared her story with us

and the other patients and their families. She talked about losing her self-esteem, and how the program helped her to understand the root of her addiction. She spoke with great authority, sounding exactly like one of the counselors! I was overjoyed, except for the fact that Carrie had taken up smoking. The counselors assured us that it was a "healthy" substitute for drugs.

There was a final meeting with all the patients and their families, where those graduating after thirty drug-free days received a leather thong, to be worn as a necklace, with a small leather knot called a monkey's fist attached to it. The monkey's fist is a knot used by mariners to help them dock a ship. PDAP had adopted it as a symbol of sobriety, representing the addict being pulled in from the sea of drugs and alcohol to a safe harbor.

I was so happy to see Carrie proudly wearing her newly earned necklace. We were thrilled that we were bringing home our now healthy Carrie Louise.

After we got home, I went on a tear and spoke at various schools about what we had gone through. Parents were contacting us in droves, miserable about their kids who were using, asking for any kind of advice and hope they could hang on to. I talked to the PDAP people in Houston, and we were successful in starting the program out in California.

The months flew by, and we became more and more secure about Carrie's recovery. On her sixteenth birthday, we presented her with a car.

She was due to receive her one-year-of-sobriety necklace soon—a more elaborately designed leather thong with the monkey's fist—and Joe and I wanted to celebrate by throwing a small reception at the church where the presentation was going to take place. When the day came Joe and I, with Jody and Erin, got to the church early, around five p.m. A lot of Carrie's friends were already there, plus a few grown-ups, friends of the family. One year! I kept thanking God over and over.

Carrie hadn't arrived yet. She was going to drive there with some schoolmates. They were several minutes late, but finally she breezed in, all smiles. She waved to us, but didn't come over for hugs. I felt a slight pang in my stomach. . . .

The presentation was quite moving, and afterward Carrie was proudly wearing her new necklace as the crowd enjoyed punch, sandwiches, and cookies. We hugged her and congratulated her.

"Mama, is it okay if my friends and I go out to celebrate tonight? I just need to go home and change first."

"Of course. Be home by ten?"

"Sure, great!"

I had hoped that Carrie would have dinner with us, but I didn't want to interfere if she wanted to be with her friends on this big day, so Joe, Jody, Erin, and I went out for an early dinner at Carmine's. When we came home, it looked like Carrie had already gone out, but the lights in her bedroom were still on. I went into her room to be sure, and my heart sank. She had taken off her one-year necklace and had tossed it on her bed. I knew right then that she had been lying to us.

That night Joe and I waited up for Carrie to come home. It was a little after eleven when we heard her car pull in the driveway. She came up the back stairs very quietly and went into her room. We knocked on her door, looked at each other, and went in. . . .

Diary entry:

> *We're sending her back to PDAP in Houston. One of the counselors is coming out here to fly back with her as a chaperone. I'm completely devastated. What does this mean? Can we never be sure of anything in this life? Must we always be walking on eggshells? Must we always be waiting for the other shoe to drop? Will I ever be happy again? Can I ever trust her again? What was that line we heard during Family Week? "How can you tell when addicts are lying?" "When they open their mouths."*

Carrie was checked into the hospital and the detox routine began all over again.

Before all this happened, I had begun work on the movie *Annie,* in which I played the role of Miss Hannigan. In a way I was grateful for the distraction. There were even times when I felt like I was having fun. (When was the last time I'd had fun?) But the very next thing I'd feel would be guilt.

Joe was busy preparing to produce *Mama's Family,* a spin-off series based on characters from our variety show, and Jody and Erin had mostly fallen silent around us. It was obvious they were angry at their father and me for sending their sister away again.

Then we got a call from PDAP saying Carrie had run away, followed by a call from Carrie herself telling us she was on her way back to L.A. She had brought some money with her and hidden it from the PDAP staff, planning her getaway before she even arrived. She had just enough cash to take a bus to California.

Carrie came back to L.A., but she didn't come home. She

stayed with "friends" somewhere in the city. I called her counselor in Houston, in tears, asking what we should do. I wanted to track her down and bring her home. I had never known such fear. Carrie was back to where she had been at the beginning of this nightmare. The counselor's advice? "Tough love! Don't let her come home while she's high. Let her hit bottom." I listened to him because I simply didn't know what else to do, but each day was a slow torment.

The filming of *Annie* came to an end, and now I was back home every day, where Joe and I were having our problems, too.

He had begun to drink again.

Diary entry:

> *First Daddy and Mama, then Joe, and now Carrie. Dear*
> *God in heaven, what next?*

At the time, we owned a condominium in Hawaii where we spent vacations, so I decided to get Jody and Erin as far away from L.A. as possible for a while. I packed our suitcases and we flew to Maui, leaving Joe and Carrie behind.

Diary entry:

> *We went to the beach today, and had dinner at the Spill*
> *and Grill. The girls must sense something's wrong between*
> *their father and me, but I keep mum about it. I don't talk*
> *about Carrie, either. The right words escape me. I'm grateful*
> *Jody and Erin have each other, because their mother is a helpless*
> *mess.*

Once Jody, Erin, and I left town, Carrie started going to the house in L.A. and visiting with Joe, bringing her laundry. She may have wanted to return home, but Joe told her she couldn't move back in while she was still getting high. After that, her visits became less frequent.

From Hawaii I spoke to Joe often, and one day he told me he was going to enter a rehab facility outside of Los Angeles. He had committed to the thirty-day program and was leaving the house in the care of our housekeeper, Gigi. I was happy that he had made that decision. Maybe he had "hit *his* bottom."

In Maui, I dreamed of Carrie every night, finding myself in different scenarios, trying to find her, not knowing how she was, or even if she was still alive. I would wake up in a cold sweat, terrified.

Diary entry:

> *Gigi called and said Carrie came by asking for money, and that she looked like death. Ashen, gaunt, rail-thin, and shaking. I have to do something NOW! I'm not going to wait until she hits bottom. No, no, no! She's my baby. As far as I'm concerned, she has "hit bottom" now!*

Carrie was seventeen, so legally Joe and I were still in charge, but that would only last until her eighteenth birthday. I called Gigi back and told her to tell Carrie that her dad would give her some money, but she would have to go to the rehab facility where he was, in order to get it. Gigi would drive her there. I then called the rehab facility, told them the story, and asked that they admit her immediately. They put me through to Joe, and I filled him in.

I hung up and waited. All hell was breaking loose in California, and here I was with Jody and Erin three thousand miles away on an island in the middle of the Pacific. I stared at the phone for over two hours waiting for a call—waiting and weeping. The girls were obviously worrying about me, but I knew they had their fears about Carrie, too. I just wasn't able to console myself at the moment, much less them.

Finally, the phone rang and the person on the other end introduced himself as Dr. Peters. He told me that when Carrie realized she had been tricked she had gone crazy and had tried to run away. She couldn't get out of the building, though, and finally they were able to restrain her. Furious, she was cursing me and calling me every name in the book, even though I wasn't there. After the doctor had calmed Carrie down, he gave her a sedative to help her sleep. We were at the beginning of yet another thirty-day program.

I knew I had done the right thing. I finally realized I had to love her enough to let her hate me.

Diary entry:

> *Exhausted, but awake. It's four a.m.*
>
> *Leaving for L.A. with Jody and Erin in a few short hours. Another "Family Week" ahead.*
>
> *Feel compelled to write, but don't know what exactly. Thinking about the time Joe and I discussed finding some underprivileged kid who got good grades but would never be able to afford a good private boarding school, and pay for his or her high school education (which we wound up doing anonymously). This came out of a discussion about Carrie and whether or*

not she could ever appreciate the opportunities that had been handed to her.

Will she straighten out this time, or will she blow it?

She's writing her own life story now. She has the potential for having and doing it all—a good brain, a sense of humor, enormous charisma, plus financial means. I'm coming to realize that this puts an extra burden on a soul, and that she needs to be extra strong to avoid succumbing to all those temptations out there. It's just too easy for someone who grew up the way she did to simply live for the many pleasures of this materialistic world. Everything she could ever ask for has just been handed to her, but if she can take these things and choose the path of giving and helping, she could accomplish so much in her lifetime.

I just realized something! For all the obvious difficulties of my childhood, I had it easier than Carrie did! I am dumbstruck by the thought. Not only did our modest means provide me with far fewer temptations, but my goal in life was crystal clear from the beginning: survival. Period. There was no room in my life for experimentation. Anything that didn't contribute to staying alive was an indulgence I couldn't afford, pure and simple.

Now I'm thinking that Carrie and kids like her (by that I mean from all outside appearances) aren't actually born into fortunate circumstances at all when it comes to developing character, or their souls. If someone heads along a good path IN SPITE OF a silver spoon in their mouth, then I believe they've really done more *hard work than someone like me, who had none of the distractions and temptations that come with those "advantages."*

God, how often do we say and hear, "I just don't get it. These kids today have so much more than we ever had. We had to work, we had no money, we had to struggle. What the hell's the matter with them? They should be so damn grateful. We certainly would be!"

Would we?

Could we have survived and made something of ourselves if we hadn't HAD to?

Odd. Suddenly I don't seem to resent these people for their "golden opportunities" now. The prostitute who gives up her way of life seems to me more blessed than the pious woman who was never tempted to use her body to make a living.

In other words, if you don't like chocolate, then you're not proving much by refusing a bonbon.

4:45 a.m.

I guess this is why I woke up. These thoughts have made some things more clear to me, and I pray they will help me to help Carrie . . . and to be more understanding and less frightened, although I know this is not over, not by a long shot.

The wee hours of quiet and solitude are precious. I know this time has been put to good use, and for this I'm grateful, too.

As Jody, Erin, and I were flying over the ocean to L.A. I thought about the strange turn of events that put my daughter and my husband in the same situation at the same time in the same hospital. I was nervous, not only for myself, but for all of us. Jody and Erin were too young to have all this stress surrounding Carrie foisted upon them, and now their father was in the mix. I closed my eyes and prayed for us all.

Dr. Peters turned out to be a very special and gifted young doctor whose expertise was in teenaged addiction. I spoke to him daily, and he said Carrie had "come around" fairly fast. That made me feel happy, but I didn't trust my happiness . . . not yet. Joe and Carrie would pass each other in the hall every day as they were going to their separate counseling sessions. It made Joe uncomfortable, but he, too, was relieved that for now Carrie was someplace safe.

After a week in L.A., Jody, Erin, and I drove for a couple of hours down to Joe and Carrie's hospital, and checked into a nearby hotel where we would stay during "Family Week." We were all on edge. The girls hadn't seen their father for over a month, and it had been longer than that since we had seen Carrie. Joe met us at the elevator, and we all hugged. Then we saw Carrie waiting for us down the hall. I flashed back to the first time we saw her after her thirty days at PDAP. And this time, too, she ran to all of us with a wide smile on her face, and tears in her eyes.

Diary entry:

> *Dare I hope? YES. I'm not going to fear the worst. I'm not going to give fear any more power over me. I'm going to hope for the best.*

Every day during "Family Week" families and patients would gather in a large room with chairs arranged in a circle. In the center of that circle two chairs were placed facing each other. The patient could only sit in one of them quietly, not saying a word, while family members would take turns sitting in the other one, pouring their hearts out. They talked about all that had happened, and how badly they wanted their loved one to get well and stay well. Family after family went into the middle of the circle. One of the most powerful feelings came from seeing that we were not alone. All of us here were going through it. There truly wasn't a dry eye anywhere in that room. The only thing that surprised me about that was discovering that I still had some tears left.

Now it was our turn. We were the only family who had two loved ones to deal with. Carrie sat in her chair and heard her younger sisters separately tell her all about their fears for her and how much they loved her. Joe spoke to her next. She took in every word, nodding and crying. Then it was my turn, and I didn't hold back, either. At the end of the session, we all embraced, and when Carrie hugged me she said, "Thank you, Mama."

Now it was Joe's turn to sit in the chair. We went through the same thing with my husband and the father of our three girls. It wasn't easy. Not only did Jody, Erin, and I have to tell him how we felt, but now Carrie had to sit in the chair opposite the one she had just vacated, facing her father and airing her own feelings about his disease, while he just looked at her and wept. It was an incredible experience. Somehow, I knew in my heart that this time Carrie would be okay.

When the week ended, we all went home together, where we had a family powwow. We all agreed that we should go public to ward off any tabloid stories with all their distortions. We wanted to tell our truth about Carrie's drug abuse, so we gave *People* magazine the story and it made the cover. Over a smiling picture of Carrie and me they ran the headline, "Carol Burnett's Nightmare," which I hated. Carrie laughed about it, calling herself "Mama's Little Nightmare."

Now that we were all back together, it became clear to Joe and me that we had grown too far apart. We decided to separate. We were worried about telling the girls, but it wasn't as difficult as we had anticipated. Although they had never mentioned it, they had suspected that their father and I had been having problems for quite a while, and even though they were sad they weren't surprised. Joe and I assured them that we would remain friends. He went back to work on the show he had been producing before his thirty-day stint in rehab, and Carrie, Jody, Erin, and I flew to the condo in Maui to spend some time healing. And heal we did.

The girls and I sunbathed and swam and hit the local malls and went to the movies. Carrie and I spent hours playing Scrabble. She wiped me out plenty of times fair and square, but she also knew how to get to me. All she had to do when it was her turn was take fifteen minutes before every move and the wait would drive me nuts. When my turn finally came I'd put down the first word that came to mind. I would lose out of sheer boredom. Anyway, that's my story (and I'm sticking to it).

For some silly reason, we gave each other fake names on the Scrabble score pad. I was "Mary" and Carrie became "Clara." When she wanted to play some more, she would pipe up, "Hey, Mary! Wanna go another round at Scrabble?" I would reply, "You betcha, Clara!" And we'd be off and running. All four of us laughed a lot during that time on the island. I had never been happier, and I knew Jody and Erin felt the same way. They had their big sister back.

We celebrated my forty-ninth birthday by spending a weekend on the island of Kauai. We went horseback riding and even took a helicopter tour, landing on a deserted beach for a picnic. We watched the sun set and flew back to the hotel with the score from *Superman* playing in the helicopter. I had my girl back—all three of them, really.

Celebrating my forty-ninth birthday in Hawaii

As a result of the *People* magazine article, Carrie and I were asked to appear on various television shows to talk about the hell we had all gone through. After those appearances we received tons of letters from parents all around the country, thanking us for shining a light on the dark secrets most families keep when they're faced with the ugliness and fear of their teenagers' addiction. Many said that our coming out of the closet helped them to stop being afraid to face, head on, the problems their kids had, to stop being afraid of them. They realized the best way through the nightmare was to face the truth, take charge, and find the courage to put their kids in a rehab facility, even if they balked. They came to the same realization I had: "You have to love your kids enough to let them hate you."

I remember being interviewed on *The Phil Donahue Show*. I had decided to accept any and all such invitations, not to offer advice, but to make myself available to answer people's questions about our experience. I appeared on *The Tonight Show* with Johnny Carson, *The Dinah Shore Show*, several news programs, radio shows, and now here I was with Phil Donahue, one of daytime's most popular television hosts, trying to help other parents. So in a way, I guess I *was* giving advice when Phil said, "On the other hand, it must have been hard at the time for Carrie to be Carol Burnett's daughter . . ." I smiled back and said, "Let me put it this way, I *wish* I'd had me for a mother." The audience applauded. I was embarrassed, but it was the truth.

Carrie, on her own, went on to speak to kids at several junior high and high schools about her drug abuse, how she got into it, and her recovery process. After one of her talks, I received a letter from the assistant principal of a special high school program in Torrance who thought I might be interested in getting some feedback about Carrie's appearance at their assembly for two thousand students. He said her message really hit home with the kids and enclosed a few of the critiques that the students wrote.

"In my opinion, I liked the way Carrie presented her speech. It wasn't formal. It was a real live person with a real live story to tell. It was never boring, and very interesting to say the least."

"I thought that the speaker was very good. She didn't bore us with a lecture, and she didn't say, 'Don't do it.' Instead, she told us about her life. She proved to me how drugs and alcohol can really put a burden on anyone's life. I would recommend that more speakers like that are brought to speak to the student body."

"I thought the assembly was outstanding. It's about time we get to listen to someone that speaks our language. She didn't give us a lot of percentages and figures. She came right out and told the blunt truth. She always had everyone's attention and she never bored you."

"This was the best assembly we've had so far. She was very honest. Perhaps her use of four-letter words was, at times, too much, but since this approach got the students' attention, it was worthwhile. This school should have more speakers like her."

"It wasn't what she said that made people listen, but the way she said it. She understood her audience completely. Some of the teachers were upset because she didn't use proper language, but personally I thought the program was worth it. She knows how to speak to 'normal' teenagers."

A year later, after getting her high school diploma by taking the GED tests, Carrie applied to Pepperdine University in Malibu and was accepted. A dear friend of the family, an adjunct faculty member, told me about the time he showed Carrie around the campus. He took her to the main theater, which was empty at the time. They stood in the back for a minute, soaking up the vibe before she took him by the hand, walked him down the aisle, and sat him in the center of the fourth row. She then climbed up on the stage, put her hands on her hips, looked around, and said, "Get used to sitting there, Uncle Bill, I'm going to be performing on this stage a lot!"

Carrie majored in Pepperdine's arts program, which included music and drama. She sang in the school's jazz band program and won the lead in a student production of *Barefoot in the Park,* which was performed in the main theater. The whole family attended and I thought she was terrific, but after all, I *was* her mother. . . .

A few weeks later, I received a letter from the director of the theater department at Pepperdine about Carrie's performance. He told me that he was very impressed with Carrie's devotion and dedication and especially her comedic timing. He said everyone loved working with her and congratulated me for having such a "pro" for a daughter.

Carrie had what people in the business call "comedy chops" and she became one of the stars in the theater department. As her dreams of acting were fulfilled, her self-esteem was reborn. I knew we had a budding artist in the family and I was thrilled for her. The "nightmare" was truly over at last.

Sadly, by this time Joe and I had gone ahead and finalized our divorce. Happily, we remained friends until his untimely death from cancer ten years later.

During the next few years, Carrie pursued her goals of acting, singing, composing music, and writing. She appeared in major motion pictures and landed roles in many television series.

Musically, she formed a couple of bands and performed in clubs around Los Angeles. She loved it all, country, folk, rock and roll, jazz . . . the whole ball of wax. The music they often played was a mix of the Who, the Rolling Stones, and Rickie Lee Jones.

In the early '90s, Carrie fell in love. He proposed, and they were married in 1994.

The wedding I threw for them turned out to be a pretty unusual event, to say the least. CBS offered us the use of Studio 33 in Television City, where we had taped our variety show for eleven years.

The marriage ceremony was going to take place up on the stage and the guests were going to sit in the audience seats. Along with family and friends, we invited many of the people who worked at CBS and had watched Carrie grow up when she, Jody, and Erin used to come to our early taping of *The Carol Burnett Show* every Friday. So this was a very special place to hold the ceremony.

Carrie had found the judge she wanted in the Yellow Pages! She showed up early, and was quite the sight—an ample older woman dressed to the nines in cobalt blue sequins, topped with a bright-red velvet turban. Trailing along behind her on a leash was her pet bulldog, Arnold. She explained that she took Arnold everywhere she went because he happened to be her reincarnated dead husband. Everybody ate up the unusual venue, and the kookiness of the judge from the Yellow Pages with her "husband," Arnold. Carrie, of course, simply adored the whole scene!

Some weeks before the nuptials, Carrie and I had gone shopping for her wedding dress. We went to the obvious bridal shops, but being Carrie, she didn't want anything that smacked of convention. So we wound up at a secondhand vintage store, and found a pretty, antique, cream-colored lace number cut low in the back, with a jacket. It suited her. I especially liked the jacket, because it covered the large tattoo of a bird-of-paradise on her right shoulder. Though it was a pretty enough tattoo, I never cottoned to the idea of permanent ink on the body. When she first had it done, I said, "Honey, this is going to be with you the rest of your life! What'll people think when you're an old lady in the old folks' home with this . . . this . . . *bird* on your shoulder?" She replied, "Mama, they won't think anything about it, because chances are good that they'll all have tattoos, too!"

Still, I was glad the jacket came with the dress.

Back to the wedding. Everyone was seated in the audience waiting for the ceremony to begin. There was an expectant tension in the air. Carrie's fiancé took his place near the judge. Arnold began sniffing and drooling on the groom's pants, and we all tried not to laugh at the thought that the next thing Arnold would do was lift his leg. Carrie didn't want the wedding march. She wanted George Gershwin. So the trio I had hired struck up Gershwin's "Our Love Is Here to Stay" as Carrie made her entrance. She had a pale-pink plume in her hair, and a matching boa around her neck. She had ditched the jacket, and the colorful tattoo on her shoulder completed the ensemble. All I could think was, "Well, that's my girl. Why am I not surprised?"

For their honeymoon, the newlyweds decided to drive all over the country in search of a "getaway," a place to recharge while they still maintained a modest home in Los Angeles. They found their dream location in the small town of Gunnison, Colorado, a little cabin on forty acres that they proceeded to renovate by adding a second-story bedroom and a new roof. Carrie learned how to wield a mean hammer. Friendly neighbors helped them and it wasn't long before they were ready to settle into their home in the mountains.

For the next couple of years, Carrie continued working on her career, going back and forth to Los Angeles to make more guest appearances on various television series and to play her music in clubs. Carrie auditioned for and got the role of Maureen in the first national company of the musical *Rent*.

It was at this point that I suspected things weren't going well in their marriage. Carrie was traveling a lot but her husband chose to remain alone in their Colorado cabin. They separated in 1998 after four years of marriage.

Carrie and I kept in touch mostly by e-mail, but since she hardly ever mentioned what went wrong with her marriage, I chose not to pry. Eventually, she opened up to me.

From: Carrie
To: Mama
Sent: Dec. 1, 2000

Well, Mama, the documents finally came through. I'm now officially divorced. It feels a little strange. I'm glad I took a long time to file and it took so long to process. As you know, we've been separated since '98! I remember how worried you sounded back then whenever we talked. I knew you

could hear it in my voice that things weren't quite right, but I
didn't want to get into it, Mama, even after I filed for divorce.
I don't know why, but I felt I had to tough it out alone, and
I'm grateful you never pushed. I still love him, but I have
little respect for the man he became over the last several
years, so I don't pine. And it feels good now to be able to
open up, knowing it's finally over.

We'd been having problems off and on, but our troubles
escalated in '96, when I got the part of Maureen in *Rent*.
This was a big deal for me, being the first national company
and all, but instead of being happy for me, he became sullen
and withdrawn. He had no job at the time, so this break was
a boon to us both, but he didn't see it that way. I asked him
to go on the road with me, but he preferred to stay in our
cabin and sulk.

How many times I've wished things had worked out. How
many times I just wished he had grown with me, instead
of against me. The sweet Dr. Jekyll he once was had been
turned into the Mr. Hyde I could no longer live with. I wonder
if I'll ever love anyone as much again. I do miss that feeling
of partnership with someone, and as much as I love my
work, you can't talk to your work—or if you do, people look
at you funny!

I love you, Mama. Thanks for being there.

C

Carrie bounced back and forth from Colorado to Los Angeles (where she picked up some acting jobs to pay the rent), but she found herself longing for her mountain retreat more and more, and began spending more time there in order to concentrate on writing.

In late 2000, Carrie was working on a new story in her beloved cabin, and began sending pages to me, at home in Los Angeles.

To: Mama
From: Carrie via FAX! ☹
Gunnison, Colorado
Dec. 3, 2000

Hi Mama,

I'm *faxing* (instead of e-mailing) you the first few scenes of a story that I'm writing, "Sunrise in Memphis." It's about a bohemian girl and the mysterious cowboy she meets, and their road trip to Graceland.

I printed out the pages just before my computer got a headache and then gave me one. I'm taking it into town tomorrow to the "Mr. Fixit" computer store. I hope the owner can create a miracle and have it up and running tomorrow or the next day. He's been pretty good at helping me out in similar situations before. Gunnison may be a small Colorado town, but it rocks!

Meantime, I'm happy that my fax machine is still healthy! ☺
Sooo . . . I hope you can read my scrawl.

It feels funny putting pen to paper, especially in this era of
"high tech," but somehow I don't think it's a bad thing when
stuff goes wrong and you have to get back to the basics.
Like actually writing an honest-to-God letter in longhand!

Sometimes I think my handwriting looks suspiciously like
yours—the way certain letters curl and dip. Just like how
my hands now look like yours—and how at certain angles it
looks like you spit and I grew. The line where you end and I
begin has always been blurry. And yet there are fundamental
differences that make us a unique team, able to balance
and complement each other.

Did you know that Steinbeck wrote *East of Eden* by hand?
In PENCIL? I'm reading it now, for the first time, and what a
fine novel it is. If you haven't read it, or haven't visited it in
a long time, please do so. It's a quick read for such a long
novel, thanks to the beauty and simplicity of his writing—
dazzling turns of phrases, but not the kind that send you
rushing for a dictionary.

Maybe my computer broke down because I needed to take
a breather. This gorgeous Colorado sky is saying, "Get your
ass out to the front porch and rock for a while. INHALE! Take
in this beautiful and rarified mountain air! Even if it hurts
your lungs!" I love my rocking chair. I love my home here,
Mama. Funny, I grew up in the city, and became a creature

of Hollywood, but I've discovered that this lover of clubs and rock and roll (and all kinds of music) with a bird-of-paradise tattoo on her shoulder, can do a 180 and relish the peace and quiet I find in my mountains. I still love my part-time life in L.A., my friends, the excitement of writing and singing new music, and doing acting jobs on TV that (thank God) pay the bills. But what I look forward to most is coming back here.

XO Carrie

To: Carrie
From: Mama via FAX
Dec. 3, 2000

Hi Baby, I got your first few pages of "Sunrise in Memphis" and plan to read them as soon as I put my contact lenses in.

I hope your computer will be up and humming along ASAP. I know how frustrating it can be when technology decides to go south. However, make no mistake, I love your "scrawl." How did we ever live without computers??? 'Twas a simpler time back in the covered wagon days when your mama here was a youngster. The good thing is that you're able to take the world in stride by going out to rock in your chair on the front porch and not let this sudden inconvenience spoil your day. I'm happy you're so happy in your mountain hideaway. And I truly admire your love of "waking up and smelling the roses."

Love, Mama

To: Mama
From: Carrie
Dec. 4
Another FAX ☹ from your still COMPUTER-LESS daughter!

The first few scenes of SUNRISE came fast, but I'm not sure where they'll be taking me.

I think about the leading character, Kate, often throughout the day, trying to pry into her head and heart and figure out what she needs to learn during the course of this story, and how she will learn it during her journey to Graceland. I know the mysterious cowboy will somehow become her teacher, and I know how the whole thing ends (I'm not gonna tell you yet!), but my challenge will be how to get there.

I'm also including a real-life friend of mine, Charles, as one of the main characters. Charles will be a running thread throughout the story. He's the doorman for the Burgundy Room (a club in Hollywood that will be featured as "flashbacks" in the story). He checks IDs and removes unruly people if needed, and gets everyone to go home when the bar closes at two a.m. A Howard University grad, he was teaching high school English when his fiancée died suddenly of a heart attack, right out of the blue, on the very day he was going to present her with a ring (all of which you will know from reading the story).

Overcome by grief, he locked himself in his house and wouldn't come out for the longest time. The owner of the Burgundy, who knew Charles from his street singing, gave him a job. He has a deep baritone voice and sometimes still sings on the street. That's how I first met him. I spied him on a corner while I was driving in Hollywood, so I parked my Jeep and walked over to listen to him. It didn't take long for me to start singing with him. We clicked immediately.

Charles lives simply and cheaply, goes into his "dark place" sometimes, over the loss of his great love, but for the most part he's a happy camper. Stationed outside the Burgundy seven nights a week he has become confidant and sage for lots of Hollywood kids, from the homeless to young urban hipsters, to artists like me, who just like to talk to him. He's my favorite street singing partner. Our duet of "Under the Boardwalk" kills!

So that's Charles. We trade books and music, stories, thoughts, and always hugs. He is the angel of Hollywood to me. I go in early some nights just to hang out with him, have a slice of pizza and a Coke. A lot of local Hollywood bands have had Charles come in and sing on their records, and you can betcher boots that if I do one, he'll be on it, too.

What wonderful friends I have.

I've been thinking about coming out to L.A. and actually taking the road trip to Graceland myself, starting from Hollywood, just like Kate does. I have so many vistas in my head, music in my ears, sensations and feelings about it that I think (hope) they will come pouring out during my journey. Her adventure will be very different from mine, but of course Kate and I are deeply *connected.*

Thank God for this place, Mama. It took me thirty-seven years to find it, but I feel I've always been a mountain girl at heart. This is my true home, and I am so very happy to be here right now. It's so quiet you could hear a field mouse fart. Now THAT'S quiet! Speaking of mice, my kitties are here this time, so I am surely rodent-free. Pee Wee is snoring next to me, his oversized Great Dane body soaking up some good ol' Vitamin D from the sunshine. It's the perfect place to write.

I love to write, Mama. I think I might love it even more than acting, or singing, or directing, which I surely love, too. And it certainly felt great to wrap up that short movie I told you I was working on, *Lunchtime Thomas.* I don't remember how much of the story I told you, but it's about this poor Mexican owner of an out-of-the-way desert motel and gas station, whose best friend, Thomas, was accidentally responsible for the deaths of the Mexican man's wife and child in a car crash. The man has forgiven Thomas, but Thomas hasn't forgiven himself, and has holed up in one of the motel rooms. It was my first writing and directing effort with Jody as my producer, and I'm very proud of how it turned out. I'm submitting it to the Latino Film Festival this year, and I'm so excited I can hardly stand it!

As far as what I'm writing now goes, maybe I love it so much because I'm doing it alone—it's just me and my ideas without the pressure of having other chefs in the kitchen. It brings me peace. I don't know if I'm good at it or not, but it definitely brings me pleasure.

Here's hoping my computer gets well soon!

Love you, Carrie

From: Carrie
To: Mama
Sent: Dec. 5, 2000
Subject: E-mail at last! (whoopee!) ☺

"Mr. Fixit" came through! My computer and printer are humming once again—a very welcome birthday present to me!

I put a candle in a cupcake today, made a wish, and blew it out. I've made up my mind to do Kate's road trip . . . sort of a happy thirty-seventh birthday to me! (And a happy "birth"-day to you too, Mama!)

From: Mama
To: Carrie
Sent: Dec. 5, 2000

Happy Birthday Baby! My thoughts go to a time before you were born. I don't remember ever telling this story to you.

It was a blistery late November afternoon in New York. You were due in about two weeks, and I looked like I was about fourteen months pregnant. Your dad and I were living in an apartment on Central Park South. I was in a cab, turning onto our street, when I spotted the newspaper stand on the corner a half block before our building.

"Hey, you can just let me out here." I wanted to buy a magazine and I figured, even though I was as big as an elephant, I could manage the half-block walk in spite of the howling wind whipping around Columbus Circle. The cab driver slowed to a stop, and I reached over the seat and paid him. The wind was whistling like the moors in *Wuthering Heights* as I got out of the cab and headed for the kiosk.

Then I felt a tug. I was being pulled backward by something. That "something" was the cab! Part of my coat had blown back, and the bottom half of it was stuck in the door I had slammed. The driver hadn't noticed, and neither had I. He had put the car in gear and was slowly (thank God!) driving up the block looking for another fare.

As for me, I was trying not to fall down and get dragged all the way to Times Square. I was "trotting" and hollering at the driver, who didn't hear me! Several people on the sidewalk were simply staring at this spectacle, frozen. Maybe they thought they were watching a slapstick movie being shot. Finally, one of the spectators hailed the driver and he stopped—right in front of my apartment building!

I opened the door, released my coat, and what came out of my mouth was, "How much more do I owe you?"

From: Carrie
To: Mama
Sent: Dec. 6, 2000

That's a great story, Mama. I love the fact that you could come up with a crazy line like that after being dragged half a block! Makes me hope that this apple hasn't fallen too far from the tree!

Meantime: *More pages!* ☺

XO, C.

From: Mama
To: Carrie
Sent: Dec. 6, 2000

Got the new pages. I'm loving this story! I find myself trying to figure out just who this "mysterious cowboy" is! Keep 'em coming!

XO

Mama

From: Carrie
To: Mama
Sent: Dec. 6, 2000

Wait, Mama, just wait. Kate and the cowboy still have a long way to go. . . .

I'm definitely going to hit the road and duplicate their journey. I'll be writing as I travel and will send you pages of "Sunrise" along the way!

XO, C

I really didn't like the idea of Carrie driving all that way to Graceland solo. I was more than a little nervous, but she assured me all would be okay. She was so excited about the project that I finally came to the conclusion that I had to trust her, and know that she would (and could) take good care of herself.

In addition to her story, Carrie was also working on a project that involved the two of us. She had called me a couple of years before, wanting us to write a play together based on my first memoir, *One More Time*. The play would feature the family I grew up in: my grandmother (Nanny), my mother (Louise), and my father (Jody).

Carrie and I wrote separately—I from Los Angeles, and Carrie from her mountain cabin in Colorado—faxing scenes back and forth. Eventually we had enough of a script to submit to the Sundance Theatre Workshop. We were accepted, and spent a happy time in Utah working together honing our story. We titled it *Hollywood Arms*, which had been the name of the apartment building Nanny and I had lived in when we left Texas and moved to California. I sent a rough draft to my friend, Tony-winning director and producer Hal Prince, for his comments and he volunteered to direct and produce our little play! We were over the moon! We decided to aim for a production in Chicago in 2002.

As part of her trip to Graceland, Carrie planned to make two additional stops as research for *Hollywood Arms*. She was going to visit my hometown, San Antonio, Texas, to see the house I lived in as a little girl. And on her way home from Memphis she planned to stop in Belleville, Arkansas, where Nanny and Mama (my grandmother and mother) were born. Carrie wanted to soak up some "family vibes" in preparation for working on our play. So I swallowed my fear and wished her Godspeed.

From: Carrie
To: Mama
Sent: Dec. 27, 2000
Subject: Surprise, Arizona

HI MAMA! WELL, I'M ON THE ROAD TO GRACELAND! It took me a while to pack up, but I'm happy I'm finally at the wheel. Arrived last night after an uneventful drive. The AZ desert is so beautiful, not quite as dramatic as Utah, but with the sun descending behind me, and new rocks to look at (I'm pretty used to the drive home to CO, so I know those rocks!), I was happy. There are a LOT of retired folks here in golf pants. This a.m. as I was hunting down a cup of coffee, I actually saw a man driving down a three-lane main street in a pretty nifty Jetson-style golf cart! Retirement is cool.

Stopped in Blythe for gas and the woman working at the counter (Lee Press-On Nails) asked if I was visiting family for the holidays. "No, I'm driving to Memphis," I replied.

"Gonna see Elvis' house?"

Yup. I'm goin' to Graceland!

Figure I'll keep going for a day or two more, then stop in San Antonio to visit the house you and Nanny lived in when you were an itty-bitty little thing, and get a nice comfortable hotel room and write for a couple of days. Right now, I'm just absorbing.

I guess Arkansas is in a bad way, weather-wise, but Texas is warm and sunny today and it should be fine driving through the southernmost route the next day or two. If not, I'll hang wherever I land. I must say I feel very happy traveling like this. Maybe I should've been a trucker. Perhaps I was a traveling minstrel in my past life. It sure feels comfortable, safe, and right. (Don't worry about me, Mama!)

Before I hit the road, I had a nice quiet Christmas in my little cabin with some of my dear neighbors and their little girl, Mavis (six), whom I'm crazy about. We sang lots of carols and played Monopoly and Charades. Little Mavis is a whiz at all kinds of games and trounced us grown-ups to a fare-thee-well! The fireplace was blazing away and the moon lit up the snow on the mountain. It was truly a breathtaking sight.

Carrie and Me

Mama, it's almost 2001!

I plan to spend New Year's in what, I hope, will be a cozy hotel room. I don't mind it at all when I'm alone at times like this. I'm alone, but I'm not lonely.

Hope this finds you well and happy, Mama. Whenever I can get an Internet connection, I'll keep you updated on my doings, and I'll send you more of Kate's and the cowboy's story.

XO, C.

From: Mama
To: Carrie Lou
Sent: Dec. 28, 2000

Hi Honey,

I'm happy your trip thus far has been good, and that you had such a magical Christmas.

It is a beautiful time of the year, and especially thrilling for little kids. Thinking about your six-year-old friend, Mavis, brings back some happy memories I had as a kid. I remembered being in the old house in San Antonio one Christmas Eve, when Nanny and I left an apple under the tree so Santa Claus would have something to eat while he was making his stops around the world. We went to bed and

53

I woke up around midnight. I smelled pipe smoke! Nanny said, "Shhh! Santa's in the house, don't scare him away!"

I could hardly contain my excitement. We waited a few minutes, and then got out of bed. I ran into the parlor and there was a half-eaten apple, and a tiny wooden Snow White doll. We went back to bed and I cuddled the doll all night, thanking Santa in my prayers. I still don't know where the pipe smoke came from!

The only time I got mad at Santa was my seventh Christmas. By this time, Nanny and I had moved to California and we were living in one room with a Murphy pull-down bed. She told me that Santa was "on a tight budget" that Christmas, and not to expect much in the way of presents. I wasn't worried one bit, because I had personally talked to Santa Claus at the Broadway Department Store on Hollywood Boulevard the week before. When it was my turn to sit on his lap, I told him I wanted a Storybook Doll (the equivalent of a Barbie, today). He had smiled at me and nodded. I just knew I was a shoo-in for that doll!

Nanny and I had a tiny scrawny tree and underneath it, on Christmas morning, not a doll was in sight. Instead there was a small package. I tore it open and there was my present from Santa . . . a white patent leather coin purse. Empty. I was surprised a moth didn't fly out.

That afternoon Nanny and I got on the bus and went to Aunt Dodo and Uncle Parker's house for turkey. I liked going over there because they had a backyard with a swing set and cousin Janice (we called each other Cuz) and I would go outside and play. That day I remember walking into their living room, where under a tall Christmas tree lay tons of opened boxes and torn wrapping paper. And there it was! A Cinderella Storybook Doll—that Santa had left for Cuz.

Boy, was I pissed! I let my hostile feelings toward Santa Claus go the way of the dodo bird about a year later, when I learned that he wasn't real.

Christmas is nice, but I always look forward to the New Year and this year is no different. Meantime, keep the "Sunrise" pages coming! Let's talk on the first.

XO Mama

From: Carrie
To: Mama
Sent: Dec. 30, 2000
Subject: San Antonio, Texas

I'm here, Mama, where you were born!

I've played my music here before, but I was in and out in one night, so I only have a very vague recollection of that visit. I got here early today after having stayed in Junction, TX, last night. Jean, the clerk at the motel (probably in her sixties), marveled at "How you kids seem to just jump in the car and drive all over. Drive, drive, drive! It's as if you want to see everything!"

Well . . . yes.

Jean was actually quite delightful. When I told her I was a writer that really got her going. She loves to read. "I go to places in my mind." So I suppose she, too, wants to "see everything," just from the safety of her Barcalounger!

I plan to stay on here until the second.

What a day! I went to the house in San Antonio where you spent your first six years. Great to know the name of the family that still lives there after all these years, and that you send them flowers every Christmas. It made it easier to ring the doorbell. The family that lives there wasn't home, but the housekeeper, Rosa, was. Her English wasn't the greatest, but she was very sweet. When I told her my mama had lived there as a child, she knew immediately who you were and was kind (and trusting!) enough to let me in.

The house was a whole lot bigger than I thought it would be, and your Christmas flowers were still in the dining room, prominently displayed! It was wild walking those halls you had walked and played in so many years ago. I remembered your telling me that you used to roller-skate on the wood floors of the slanted hallway. Well, guess what? The skate marks are STILL THERE!!! Rosa told me that they had tried to buff them out but to no avail. I was happy that I got to see them.

There were family photos on the mantel, and when Rosa was showing me the daughter, Fita, she began to cry. Fita died almost a year ago from cancer. It was so sad. Rosa cried the whole rest of the time I was there, and I hugged her tight and told her that Fita was with God and it's all okay for her now, it's just sad for those of us left behind. What a kind, openhearted lady. I'll never forget her.

Love, Carrie

San Antonio house with a recent facelift

I was so pleased that Carrie paid a visit to the old San Antonio house, and had been invited in for a special tour by Rosa. I had given her the address before she left Gunnison to go on this trip. Nanny and I had left San Antonio for Los Angeles when I was seven, but I still remember skating on the cracked sidewalk in front of the house, falling down, skinning my knees, and screaming bloody murder when Nanny was hot on my trail with the iodine. After several of these mishaps Nanny decided that I should roller-skate *inside* the house on the hallway that led to the front screen door (retiring the iodine bottle for good, much to my relief). This, needless to say, was the time when I contributed the permanent skate marks to the floor.

The roller skate marks I made in 1937 are still there!

From: Carrie
To: Mama
Sent: Dec. 31, 2000
Subject: NEW YEAR'S EVE!!!

Tonight I hear they have fireworks and bands by the Riverwalk Hilton, not too far from where I'm staying. I may walk over later (bundled up, it's in the thirties) if I feel like it. The fresh air and exercise will be good for me after four days on my butt in the car. I jimmied the window in the room so that it could open. I hate hotels with windows that don't open, so I brought my trusty screwdriver with me to undo the locks. (I'm very good at it and don't leave any marks!) Other than that, I'm very happy I threw down for a nice hotel (not a $26 motel) if for no other reason than room service. The food on the road is wretched and this way if I get going with writing, I don't have to leave for any reason. Besides, I'm a sucker for the water glass with the plastic wrap over the top.

Hope you're having a fine New Year's Eve doing whatever makes you happy. I so prefer being alone on nights like these. Wonder why? I *do* miss my friends and family, and the awareness of being a woman traveling alone never leaves me, but for some reason I like being off my footing a little.

I thought maybe I would be jotting down significant emotional experiences on the road, but so far I've just felt content and happy to be moving. It's a kind of basic, animal thing. I'm sure that has to do with just driving. Even with what I call "dawdling" on the road, I managed to get a speeding ticket. (Don't worry, Mama, I've slowed down.)

Last night, I went to a café that looked very local and had a huge WELCOME HUNTERS sign out front. I'm not unfamiliar with that kind of thing in Colorado, but walking into a place like that you never know what you're going to find. It was very busy. The warmth between the people who ran the place (looked to be a family operation) and the diners was palpable. Reminded me of home. And I found it made me feel good instead of blue. I genuinely like people a whole lot, and it seems to me that no matter what our differences may be, we have much more in common than the beliefs that separate us.

I've always felt that we're really just part of one larger entity. . . .

Love, Carrie

"Mama, something weird just happened to me." After having been in her room for a while, Carrie had come into the den downstairs with a peculiar look on her twelve-year-old face.

"What, honey?"

"I left my body."

"What?"

"It scared me."

"What happened?"

"Lotsa times, I stare into the mirror and the room all around me goes away. Everything gets still and all I see are my eyes. That's not the scary part. But this time I felt myself *leave* my body and I wound up floating over my right shoulder, and then I was looking down at *myself* looking into the mirror."

"What were you scared of?"

"That I would float away and never come back into my body again." She began to cry and I hugged her.

"But, honey, you did pop back, didn't you?" Carrie nodded and I hugged her harder, and said, "And you know what? I think you might've had a very exciting thing happen to you just now."

"I don't know. What?" The tears were still flowing down her cheeks.

"Let me tell you something, Carrie Lou. This is pretty wild. I haven't thought about it in years, but I would do the very same thing when I was around twelve or thirteen."

"Honest?"

"Honest! I used to do it a lot. Almost every day! If I stared really hard into the mirror, I would 'leave myself' and wind up looking down at myself, just like you did, but then whenever I asked out loud, 'What am I doing? What's this all about?' I would suddenly swoop back into my body and the experience would be over. Then one day I couldn't do it anymore. I tried and tried, but it just stopped happening."

"Weren't you ever scared?"

"Not really. Maybe just a little."

"So what is it, Mama? Is it just us, or does everybody do it?"

"I wouldn't be surprised if other people have the same experience, because you know what? I think we're all alike, and that all of us are the same underneath. That we're all ONE."

"Really?"

"I remember another time when something weird like this happened to me, but it happened only once. I was about five years old and Nanny and I were living in the old house back in San Antonio. I would go into the tiny backyard almost every day, and lie down on the grass to look up at the clouds. This one day it was very hot. I even remember what I was wearing—a little blue halter top and shorts.

"As I was lying there, trying to find faces in the clouds, something extraordinary happened. I don't know how long I had been staring up at the sky, but I found myself *floating* up toward it. I just kept floating higher and higher. It was as if I wanted to be a part of the clouds, or one of its faces."

"Were you scared?"

"No, I don't know why, but for some reason I wasn't. I think it was because I felt at that very moment that I was everything in the universe and everything in the universe was in me. I felt completely safe. I was just a little kid, but I've been hoping for that feeling to come back my whole life, honey."

By this time Carrie had stopped crying.

I went on, "It made me believe that there was more to this world than just what we can see . . . that human beings are all connected, no matter where we live in this world, or what language we speak. As a result of that hot afternoon when I soared up into the sky, I felt like I wasn't alone in this world, whatever it is, and that we're all part of something greater. So you really got a very special gift today. Don't be afraid, be grateful."

Carrie smiled and hugged me.

I often think about that afternoon the two of us shared all those years ago. I certainly don't think we're the only people who have had similar experiences. In fact, I know we're not. I believe it's possible that these things happen to every one of us on this Earth, but maybe mostly when we are quite young, so we don't always remember. At that age, grown-up rules haven't had time enough to interfere.

From: Carrie

To: Mama

Sent: Jan. 1, 2001

Subject: HAPPY NEW YEAR!!

Was up late last night, watching the ball drop on TV. Since I have no TV at home in Colorado, it's always fun to watch in hotels—it's a guilty pleasure.

It was good to hear your voice tonight. HAPPY NEW YEAR!

I began to work on "Sunrise" again and more pages flowed easily and readily last night and this morning. What a relief. I just pray that I have more in me. I thought I had avoided putting any of myself into this story, but now I'm seeing that I have to marry my feelings and experiences with Kate's. I've started to see her as I was when I was in my twenties, which makes it easier for me to get into her head. I'm not sure where her adventure with the cowboy is going from here, but I know the feeling I wish to evoke.

I've also come to the conclusion that the act of writing is almost as important to me as the result (not a bad way to look at it, or at life, for that matter!).

XO, C

To: Carrie
From: Mama
Sent: Jan. 1, 2001

Happy New Year, Honey! Got your pages. Loved the church scene where everyone was happily singing gospel music. I missed out on that kind of churchgoing in my youth.

Whenever we'd go to church everyone seemed to be so
damn serious all the time. I never got it when someone
would say, "I really enjoyed today's sermon." It sure didn't
look like it to me!

Going to church with Nanny on Sunday mornings was
something else entirely. WOW. I remember hitting the
Christian Science Church on Hollywood Boulevard. Nanny
would go to the service for the grown-ups, while all of us
little ones would be herded downstairs to the basement to
read Bible stories. I was probably seven, and at that age
I hated being separated from Nanny because I was afraid
she might drop dead on me. Even though she claimed to
be a Christian Scientist she was constantly feeling her
pulse, complaining that her heart was skipping beats. If her
symptoms didn't improve after quoting sections of Mary
Baker Eddy's *Science and Health with Key to the Scriptures,*
she would ask me to give her the bottle of phenobarbital
she kept as backup. She would pop one or two pills and
then conk out for an hour or so.

I remember one Sunday when I decided to skip Sunday
school and sneak upstairs to locate Nanny's whereabouts in
church. She had made me a navy blue felt hat that sported
a red feather that stuck way up in the air. I opened the big
doors into the main area of the church, promptly got down
on all fours, and began to crawl down the center aisle
looking from left to right at everyone's feet. That way I could
see if she had keeled over on the floor during one of her
spells.

Then I figured if Nanny *had* keeled over, nobody would know it in church because a good Christian Scientist never gets sick; they'd just think she was taking a nap. I was beginning to panic because I hadn't found her yet. I was about to scream for her when someone spotted me and piped up, "Why, look at the little Indian!" The whole congregation began to laugh, and I started to cry. Nanny popped up out of the blue and ushered me out of there. As happy as I was to see her, I cried even louder.

"Now what's the matter?"

"Everybody was laughing at me!" I was mortified.

Nanny said, "They weren't laughing at you; they were laughing at that big red feather sneaking down the aisle."

Now, of course, I love it when I can get a laugh—and it's mortifying when I don't!

From: Carrie
To: Mama
Sent: Jan. 2, 2001
Subject: Lafayette, Louisiana

Dear "Little Indian!"

I think I'll go to the mall tomorrow and look for a hat with a red feather!

From: Carrie
To: Mama
Sent: Jan. 3, 2001
Subject: Lafayette, Louisiana

Stores here in Lafayette open at noon, but I was there at eleven, just walking around with the folks that make it their home. A lot of homeless people crash at this mall at night, which is a good thing as it's very cold here right now, and the idea of sleeping outside is horrific.

My hair appointment at noon was with a nineteen-year-old girl (Rosie) who has a one-year-old daughter out of wedlock with her boyfriend. They're all living with her mother, and Rosie is "so over" this guy, who sounds like a bit of a pill.

He is only twenty-three, but he's already divorced and has a child from his previous relationship! To top it off, he's the jealous type, drives Rosie crazy and she has put up with this nonsense since she was sixteen.

Listening to her I felt like she could've been me at that age. We talked about boundaries and choices and what's better for her daughter to see: a mommy who has clear boundaries and strong self-esteem OR a mommy who compromises and finally gives up. No contest, but in matters of the heart, we can sometimes make very poor choices. It's complicated, of course, but I wanted to SHAKE her and say for godsakes quit having babies while YOU'RE still a baby! You're only

NINETEEN! And she feels it, seeing her friends go out, have fun, etc., while she has very grown-up responsibilities. I felt for her, and was so grateful that I've finally, *finally* realized that I don't have to put up with any horseshit from anybody anymore. AMEN!

It was nice to sit and talk with someone beyond just "Here's your change, have a nice trip." After a few days of that, my exchange with Rosie seemed like a conversation with Noël Coward.

I like it when people open up to me, even when it's a sad tale. I feel for all the homeless folks pushing their shopping carts with all their worldly belongings around the mall. Funny, for some reason I never thought the South got this cold. I wish there were no homeless people in the world, Mama, but if there have to be, I wish they could at least live where it's warm.

I remember one time when I was in New York. It was snowing, and a homeless man asked me for some money. His coat was threadbare and his gloves were missing a couple of fingers. I did my usual thing and told him I would give him five dollars if he told me his story. He had been a singer in his youth and had dreamed of being in the opera. He had hit on hard times and now he eked out a living singing on street corners—lots of arias. Even though he was old and his voice was shot, he managed to earn just enough to keep him going. I asked him why he didn't invest in a bus ticket and head for a more welcoming climate. Florida,

perhaps. He could just as easily sing on street corners
there. And he looked at me like I was crazy and said, "What,
and miss out on all this culture???"

My hair is now black again, Mama, no purple tint just black,
black, black. Most of my friends think it's a good color
for me (which makes you the only one who doesn't feel
that way). But don't despair, Mama, I can always go back
to blond or red or whatever. You know me, my hair color
changes like the weather in Kansas!

Interesting, I've never felt totally comfortable in Texas,
even though so many of our roots are there. As soon
as I crossed the Louisiana border, however, I felt happy,
ecstatic!! Louisiana. Even the name is musical. The skies
were amazing today, dark, ominous clouds surrounded by a
ring of pale blue turning to orange and pink as the sun was
going down.

It was dark when I hit Lafayette and I didn't feel like pushing
on to Baton Rouge. Instead of finding my Days Inn, I
decided to drive into the center of town. Noticing a virtually
abandoned Hilton, my brain went right to room service
(spoiled!) and a peaceful night at the computer. Now I'm
enjoying some spicy gumbo and crawfish pies (mmmm) and
will attempt to write. I promise not to stray from the Days Inn
anymore (the Hilton is nice, but not any nicer, and PRICIER!).

It's been quite a journey, so far. Seeing the house, meeting
that sweet Rosa, and now in Louisiana on my way to Baton

Rouge and points beyond. I should be in Memphis by
Thursday.

The scenes are coming fast. Will send several more pages
soon.

Love you. C

From: Carrie
To: Mama
Sent: Jan. 4
Subject: Greenville, Miss.

Wow, Mama! I thought it couldn't get any better. My mind is
now wandering just like it does in the isolation of Colorado,
ideas and images are popping up all over the place. Today
was almost too much to write about after eight hours at
the wheel. I left Lafayette and got lost heading out for
Greenville, and came upon an old gas station: SOUL FOOD
AND GAS. (Is that great or what? I think I'll incorporate it
as one of the stops Kate and the cowboy make during their
road trip.) Part of it had been converted into a small record
store called House Rockers Record Shop.

Stopped in and asked the saleslady for some "back porch
music," meaning foot stompin' on the boards with one guitar
and two guys splitting a 40 of "Olde E" malt liquor, or maybe
some white corn whiskey. She laughed. Nope, she had none
of that. So I loaded up on Steve Earle, Little Axe, and Lyle

Lovett, plus a CD called *Blues in the Mississippi Night.* I had a good day of music ahead.

If you were to stop and be a "tourist," take lots of pictures, etc., this trip could and should take about a year. I only have a few more days, which doesn't seem like that long anymore.

Greenville is like any other port town with gambling. I'm staying at a Comfort Inn as the Days Inn looked sketchy. I stopped at a Papa John's to get my pizza fix and there was a group of deaf people there, about eight in all, old and young (very young, about three), black and white, all signing to one another. Made me think of Jody, wishing she was with me 'cause she signs pretty well. There was a little boy there (around seven or eight) who became fascinated with me 'cause I kept making funny faces at him, and then he began to sign to me. I only know a few signs, thanks to Jody, but they're all dirty. So I opted for the universal wave. He stopped being interested, seeing as how I was illiterate.

I do believe I am in love with Mississippi and Louisiana. Listening to the CD of the old blues guys shooting the shit and talking about experiences they've had and heard about, how the blues came about, and how difficult it has been and still is to be black in America, it's something I have no idea about (being a white girl). But here in the heart of it all, as a female traveling alone, I have caught a very small glimpse of the South, hearing the voices, seeing the faces, driving by the places where so much pain was caused and so much emotion was stirred up.

Carrie and Me

I smile at everyone. (Because I want to.) The manager at Papa John's Pizza offered me a free Coca Cola as I was waiting. I thought that was mighty nice. I'm all a-jumble right now thinking about this history.

It just hit me that I honestly have no interest in visiting the plantation houses. I felt so strange when I went to Santa Fe a few years back, as if I were treading on the souls of dead Indians. I hated it there. It made me feel agitated, edgy, quick to anger. I'm sure that the old P. houses are probably gorgeous, but at what price for glory?

I heard someone on Mississippi talk radio going on about the possible change in the flag and how, although he claimed not to be racist in the least, he feels that if someone can walk around with a Malcolm X T-shirt, why can't he drive around with a rebel flag in his truck? It's all too much, and I doubt that we'll see any kind of real healing in our lifetime. These memories, our legacy, will go on and on, passed from generation to generation, hatred for no reason other than skin color (on both sides). The mistrust. The sadness. The guilt. The anger. It makes me want to cry a Mississippi River's worth of tears for us all.

Time to wash up and crawl into bed. Will send some more pages to you tomorrow.

From: Carrie
To: Mama
Sent: Jan. 5, 2001
Subject: MEMPHIS!!!

I'm here! However, the hotel room I stayed in last night in Greenville was absolutely gross. Whoever was there just before me must've had a horrific case of B.O. I opened the windows as wide as they'd go, but it didn't help much. Happy to get out of there this morning. I hopped onto Highway 61 and headed toward Clarksdale and the "crossroads of the blues."

When I got to town, I found the Delta Blues Museum. Walking in, I was greeted by a Eudora Brown, who looked to be in her twenties, and an old man in a VERY nice suit. He looked to be an old blues man for sure—almost like he was a plant, his look was so perfect.

Since I was the only other person there, I had time and space to read everything, look at everything, and absorb it all.

Clarksdale is the epicenter of Delta Blues, and at the juncture of Highways 49 and 61. A sign made of two blue guitars announces this fact. Robert Johnson, Muddy Waters, John Lee Hooker, Howlin' Wolf—they've all been here, played here, and one was even poisoned here! Ol' Robert Johnson didn't heed the advice not to let the women in the bars he played in mess with his good sense. He had a wild streak, that one, and was quite the ladies' man.

As the story goes, one evening he began flirting with a woman at a dance, who happened to be the wife of the juke joint owner. When the bartender offered Johnson the better part of a bottle of whiskey, fellow blues legend Sonny Boy Williamson allegedly advised him never to drink from a bottle that had already been opened. But Johnson replied, "Don't ever knock a bottle out of my hand." That night Johnson felt ill and had to be helped back to his room, where he died early the next morning. The whiskey had been laced with poison. Ol' Robert Johnson was twenty-seven.

It was all there, Mama, wonderful anecdotes about the men and women who changed the sound of American music forever. Most of the stories were so tragic, like Big Mama Thornton dying penniless in a boarding house in Hollywood while Janis Joplin was becoming famous covering her songs. The list goes on and on.

I dawdled in the museum for a while, and then went back into the foyer where Eudora Brown was presiding, alone. She offered to show me a video, but I didn't want to sit there and watch TV. She said, "Well, I have a selfish motive, Miss. It gets kinda lonely here. There's no one to talk to." So I said, "Well, why didn't you say so? I don't need to sit here and watch a video. We can talk!" And talk we did.

She had the most glorious smile, even with braces on her teeth. Eudora lives with and takes care of her mother, who beat cancer last year, and Eudora's dating a no-good man who's constantly borrowing money from her. She used to have a visitor at the museum who worked for Habitat for Humanity. He was polite and friendly and visited the museum quite a lot—so much so, that Eudora got the feeling that he had a crush on her. He'd come in and buy one small item and talk with her. He kept coming back time after time, and they'd talk and talk. But he never asked Eudora out, and I'm guessing he was just too shy.

He was living in Clarksdale, but he moved to San Antonio a year ago, and Eudora hasn't heard from him since. Mama, I watched her face light up when she talked about that man, and fall completely when she started talking about the man she was seeing now.

So I couldn't help myself, I just piped up and said, "Eudora, I don't know you from Adam, but your entire face changes when you talk about the man who moved to San Antonio. Why don't you look him up? Call Habitat here and see if they have a number for him! Maybe he's still single? Maybe not, but you never know."

Her eyes shone like big marbles.

"Really? Should I? Maybe I will!"

I said, "Do it TODAY! Do it NOW! I'll wait here."

This girl has taken care of her mom her entire life, and now she thinks just maybe it's "time for Eudora." I told her I agreed with her 100 percent, as long as her Mama knows that she loves her and will be there for her when she needs her and will take care of her. I think any mother worth her salt only wants to see her baby happy. And that means "time for Eudora."

So Eudora got on the phone right then and there. The director of Habitat was out, but at the end of our visit Eudora promised me she'd keep trying. We hugged, and I got in my Jeep and headed out.

Maybe I stuck my nose in where it didn't belong but Mama, I just couldn't help myself, and Eudora seemed so happy when we waved good-bye. I pray it all works out for her.

From: Mama
To: Carrie
Sent: Jan. 5, 2001

You know what, honey? Even if it doesn't work out for Eudora, maybe you helped her realize she doesn't have to put up with someone who treats her poorly. Just got your new pages. I find that I'm constantly curious as to where Kate and the cowboy are headed next.

Love, Mama

From: Carrie
To: Mama
Sent: Jan. 5, 2001
Subject: Memphis

Driving to the hotel, my thoughts wandered to Hollywood (the show business part). Somehow I was reminded of this great quote about the nurse in Shakespeare's *Romeo and Juliet.* The scholar Henry Hudson said: "She knows less than nothing of love and marriage, because she has worn their prerogatives without any feeling of their sacredness." I was thinking about just how much of that there is in Hollywood, with its so-called artists and people who want to be famous (that hollow goal)! Oh, how I love the singer that hits a clam with conviction simply because (s)he's so wrapped up in telling the story that hitting a sour note is no big deal.

Sacredness. What do you hold sacred, Mama? That's such a great question to pose to ourselves. I'll think on it further, but my immediate response is: *"That last shred of integrity."* Now there's a word!

Later, Mama.

XO

From: Mama

To: Carrie

Sent: Jan. 5, 2001

I'm not exactly sure what I hold sacred. So many things, when I think about it. Certainly love and those I hold dear. Integrity is a good one. I like to think I have it. I've never *purposely* harmed anyone, although I don't think you can get through this life without hurting some people. I remember a quote I read a long time ago, that expresses something I'd like to achieve in this lifetime: "Untouched by triumph, and untroubled by failure."

From: Carrie

To: Mama

Sent: Jan. 6, 2001

"Untroubled by failure . . ." Hmmm.

I remember being crazed over a particularly bad review I got for that TV movie you and I did together, *Hostage*. I think that's why I quit acting for a long while and plunged into my music. I was *seriously* "troubled by failure." How wrong I was to focus on the negativity of it all. Not that I regret doing music, it's just that I hate the idea of letting one person's opinion scare me off. I'm happy to say I've learned to please myself first in everything I tackle!

This trip just gets better and better. Coming into Memphis there's a HUGE billboard with the hand and bejeweled sleeve of Elvis pointing to the right that says: GRACELAND (with directions). I've booked a room at the Peabody, a very nice hotel just two blocks from where all the blues clubs are. I'll go there tomorrow. Tonight I want to write and order room service again. There's a fraternity staying here (oh Lord), but not anywhere near my room. It's blissfully quiet AND I can open the windows without using my screwdriver!

Love,

Carrie

P.S. More pages SOON!

From: Carrie
To: Mama
Sent: Jan. 6, 2001
Subject: Memphis

I'm finding that these past few pages I sent to you (where Kate meets the old blind lady, Emma Dee), are like a spun web for me. I'm afraid to tear it with cheap sentimentality. I hope I described Emma Dee's love for her dead husband in a way that others will find true.

One page at a time. I'm trying to define what true love is, or what it could be. I'm not sure if I have ever felt it, and if I have, it wasn't for very long. I was so in love when I was married, and I really thought—in my heart of hearts—that we would be together forever. But I can see now how arrogant I was to think that romantic love was all we needed, that we were somehow above the need to do the tedious, risky business of actually working through things.

Love is not arrogant, so it must be humble, I figure. So often we're too young for it.

I know the scene with Emma Dee put a lump in *my* throat, but I'm a bundle of mushy sentiment sometimes.

Love you.

Carrie

From: Mama
To: Carrie
Sent: Jan. 6, 2001

Some folks put down sentiment as too corny . . . too mawkish, too melodramatic. I'm sentimental, too, and I don't apologize for it. Keep the scene as it is. Love, Mama.

From: Carrie
To: Mama
Sent: Jan. 7, 2001

I don't apologize for it, either! Cynicism bores the hell out of me! Thanks, Mama.

Now, guess what? Today I got a chance to do something that I'll bet not too many people in this whole wide world have ever done. I rode in an elevator with five ducks. Yep, that's right.

The Peabody is known for its "Famous Ducks," which swim in the fountain in the middle of the lobby daily from eleven a.m. 'til five p.m., when they return to their penthouse apartment on the roof of the building. When the bellman was telling me about them, I got so excited that he asked if I wanted to accompany them. Turns out he's also the duck master, complete with a duck stick. Well naturally I began thinking what on earth does one WEAR to walk around with ducks?

I threw my fuchsia boa on over my outfit and came down to the lobby a few minutes before five. Caitlin, the bellman, had his "duck stick" at the ready and told me it would be about six more minutes. The lobby was PACKED with people and their cameras waiting to see the daily march of the ducks. The center elevator was open, a red carpet laid out, and steps led down from the fountain. One beautiful mallard and four brown ducks were swimming around in this very nice fountain crowned by a humongous bouquet of exotic flowers.

Really.

At five exactly, the clock in the lobby chimed, and I kid you not, the ducks (all on their own) exited the fountain, stood on the ledge, and shook themselves off. Then some very grand marching music began and a voice announced, "Ladies and gentlemen, the march of the ducks!" And without any help from the duck stick, the little buggers waddled down the steps from the fountain and paraded down the red carpet. People were taking pictures from all angles, and no lie, the friggin' ducks would look left then right and *pose* for the cameras! Julia Roberts couldn't have done it better.

Honest, Mama, I'm not kidding! AND I got to walk behind them (like some kind of publicist) and stand in the elevator while everyone got their last snapshots in. The mallard posed one last time, the doors closed, and whammo. It was just us . . . chickens. The hotel roof is vast and looks out over the Mississippi and the bridge. The ducks live in a duck-sized replica of the hotel, which includes a smaller version of the fountain, all laid out on AstroTurf. It was all too much. I was laughing the whole time.

I can't believe it's already nine-thirty. I should get some food in me and try to relax. I'm so excited, but I really don't want to go out tonight. I've already written several more pages, and I'd like to add a few more before I send them off to you.

GRACELAND tomorrow! Wow. I'll bid you adieu for now and I hope you're doing fine. I love you. You know that, don't you?

C

From: Mama
To: Carrie
Sent: Jan. 7, 2001

I'm having a swell time picturing you in your boa strutting alongside Donald and Daffy!

From: Carrie
To: Mama
Sent: Jan. 8, 2001

Today I've reached Kate and the cowboy's final goal. GRACELAND!!!

Mama, you'd get such a kick out of this place. Graceland is a cash cow not to be believed. Being a proud member of AAA I got a $1.60 discount on my admission to the mansion tour and was quickly herded onto the van, given a set of earphones for an audio tour, and shuttled up to the house.

The Christmas decorations are still up, including a HUGE manger, complete with baby Jesus, Mary, Joseph, and the three wise men, etc. In 1957 Graceland was bought along with the thirteen acres surrounding it by Elvis for $100,000 cash. They probably make that in a couple of days there now. There are visitors everywhere. I heard one woman say the tour reminded her of the Sistine Chapel. Hmmm.

I am a lousy tourist. This I know. I'm more interested in people and music and food than I am in museums and buildings, but Graceland did get to me in many ways. First off, the DÉCOR! Elvis sure did live that rock and roll legend lifestyle to the hilt, and for that I applaud him. No one today has the balls except maybe Puff Daddy.

The mix of '50s and '70s styles was great, and naturally I was taken most with the '70s stuff—the jungle room in particular with its fake fur and carved wood furnishings, complete with green shag carpet on the floor AND the ceiling! Also, the yellow and navy blue basement bar was great. One bedroom had a round, white fake fur bed complete with a half dome canopy also made out of white fur that had a built-in stereo. NOW THAT'S A BED!

Besides the wild furnishings I was most impressed with all the gold and platinum records, and various awards. There's a hallway lined with them. Takes your breath away when you realize the scope of his success, of how he really did change a generation, scaring the bejesus out of parents everywhere, just like the Beatles, the Stones, and many bands to come. That's why I laugh when people freak on Marilyn Manson and the like. It's just Elvis with contact lenses (and not nearly as much talent), but the fear of the older generation (which we are all fast becoming!) is the same. Rap music, anyone?

I became aware of Elvis when he was on the decline, so I have no real memory of him in his heyday. Baby sister Erin

was a school chum of Lisa's in grade school, remember?
And Erin actually ate Cocoa Puffs with the King! I know
Lisa Marie has had to bear quite a burden being the only
daughter of our greatest pop icon. She can't go anywhere
without people knowing who she is and having preconceived
notions about her. I think that's sad. I pray that she is
happy. I bumped into her in L.A. several months ago and we
had the grooviest conversation. She is tremendously poised,
funny, and sharp as a tack. I like her.

On the way back to the main gate in the van, I saw graffiti
ALL over the bricks and stone of the gateposts and walls.
I found that at once tragic and lovely, like so many things I
see. People love Elvis so much; he touched so many lives,
and yet to vandalize the home he lived in seems very odd to
me, but I suppose these people feel that they have a right
to have some kind of direct contact with their icon. You met
him, didn't you?

From: Mama
To: Carrie
Sent: Jan. 8, 2001

Yep. Sure did, in 1958. It was during my second appearance
on *The Ed Sullivan Show*. Elvis had just joined the army, and
the Sullivan show mounted this humongous musical salute
to him. The audience was packed with teenage girls and
their screams drowned out the huge marching band that

was part of the spectacle. Then Elvis came on, did his thing, and the place went nuts.

I don't know why, but maybe they put him on first because he had to get back to the base or something, because it was a live show. But for some insane reason, they scheduled your mama here, to *follow* . . . The King!? OMIGOD!!

I would like to tell you that my little nightclub routine "killed," but au contraire, the people in the audience just sat there and stared at me. They looked like a friggin' oil painting! The rest of the hour was one big dud. HOWEVER, I'm happy to report that, before the show, I was able to get Elvis's autograph, and he was very sweet.

From: Carrie
To: Mama
Sent: Jan. 9, 2001

Wow, Mama. I wouldn't have wanted to be in your shoes. Still, that had to be some trip!

Now about the gift shop(s) at Graceland. Yes, there are several, and I got a bunch of stuff for a few people that I knew would trip out over some kitschy memorabilia. As I was paying, I noted that a CARRIE Graceland key chain was still on the counter, and I asked the lady if she had charged me for it. An older Filipino woman standing there next in line said, "No, that's mine." I took a beat and said, "That's MY name." And she said, "MINE, TOO!" Naturally, we had to chat. She's from the Philippines, but lives on Oahu now. I told her a close friend of our family has land in Hana, Maui, but she said she doesn't like it there. "No malls." Hmmm.

Got in my car to head out. Now the funny thing is, they're doing tons of highway construction and on my way in here it took me several attempts going back and forth on the 55 to actually FIND Graceland. I thought, jeez, I've come this far, all the way to Memphis, and I can't find Graceland!?!? Finally, I did, but when I was leaving the same thing happened in reverse and I kept RE-finding Graceland! Now I couldn't get AWAY from it! I had to laugh out loud at each attempt.

Last night was interesting. I went on a "blues hunt" down Beale Street, looking for catfish and some good music. I wound up at the Blues City Café where I had a catfish sandwich, which tasted great. Bottom feeder or no, I love catfish. Why, Mama, why am I ALWAYS HUNGRY?

Beale is kind of like this Universal City walk of blues and clubs and drunks, but the musicianship is VERY high. The first club I went to, I stood next to Walter, an older cat who lives close by. He was surprised when I introduced myself and asked his name, "I haven't had a young lady introduce herself to me in about thirty-five years!" He was very funny and nice, and said, "You know who you remind me of? Carol Burnett! In her younger years, y'know, but you got them

Bette Davis eyes!" (I was pleased with the compliment, Mama, but I didn't let on.) Walter, whose nickname is "Slim," told me I could get into another club up the street called B.B.'s for free if I mentioned his name. So I did.

B.B.'s had the best sound system of all the clubs I went to. The band that night was a Prince cover band, and I hung out and talked with them for a while afterward. All really nice guys, pros who tour constantly. A couple of them, Dale and Paul, escorted me back to the hotel, which was nice. Even though it was late in a downtown area, I felt totally safe. Every man I met was a complete gentleman. It was a good night, if not necessarily the night of music I had hoped for. But I know that it's rare just to meander into town and happen upon something wonderful. But once again, the Southern hospitality was thick and much appreciated.

I cannot for the life of me understand why some people go through life being unfriendly or not taking the risk to smile when they walk into a room . . . it makes the whole world open up to you.

I know the thing I have of most value to wear isn't an expensive dress but my smile, my humor, and the very real fact that I like people and feel joy on a daily basis.

Well, it's off to the third big stop on my road trip: Belleville, Arkansas, where Nanny and your mama were born.

Love, C

From: Carrie

To: Mama

Sent: Jan. 10, 2001

Subject: BELLEVILLE, ARKANSAS!!

Mama, today was absolutely the best day yet—so unbelievable that I don't think I can describe it accurately, but I'll give it the ol' college try. I left Memphis early this a.m. feeling happy and excited to get back on the road. The hotel employees were all so great, and I had a wonderful time there. Didn't get to say good-bye to the ducks since they were still chillin' in their penthouse when I checked out.

I hit the road, crossing the mighty Mississippi again and drove right into Arkansas. Once I started to get into the Ozarks, it got very beautiful. This amazing country has so much to offer us, especially if you go off the beaten path a bit. I turned off the 40 and down the 7 by a town called Russellville, then west on the smaller country Route 10.

There it was: Belleville. Population 371. A wink of a town with one café (the Memory Lane), one store that sold everything from overalls to groceries to 2x4's, one beauty parlor (Ruth's), and a railroad crossing (that's how a lot of the town got settled). The town is surrounded by trees and quaint, well-kept homes. As I drove in I spotted a bunch of old geezers hanging out at an equally old gas station (out of service), and one of them was fixing a tractor tire.

I parked, and asked the guy fixing the tire if he knew anywhere
I could go in town to look up the birth records of a couple of
people born in Belleville. "Who you looking for?" he asked.
When I said the Joneses and the Meltons, the oldest man
in the bunch, who turned out to be Mr. Turnbull, said "I knew
them Meltons. When I was a kid I used to make fun of Henry
for bein' so old. Now I'm older than he was!!"

And we were off and running. . . .

Belleville, Arkansas, Main Street

I remembered telling Carrie that according to family lore, Herman Melton, Henry's younger brother, was supposedly my
mother's secret father, and therefore my real grandfather. I say

"supposedly" because my grandmother, Nanny ("Mae" in her younger days), may have lied on my mama Louise's birth certificate for reasons that still remain a family mystery. Seems Nanny had a checkered past.

Now that I had found myself a real live Belleville-ian, I asked a ton of questions.

Mr. Turnbull was mighty old but he told me he knew Nanny when he was a little kid or maybe just her legend, because even Duane (who looked to be in his late sixties) chimed in and said, "Oh, yeah, we've all heard the stories about Mae. She's famous 'round these parts. Quite a character. She even named herself 'The Belle of Belleville.' She was already married to Big Bill Creighton, a railroad man, when she took up with Herman Melton. She was purty much older than he was, an' she was teachin' him the piano."

Another old man piped up saying, "I think she taught him more than how to tickle the ivories!" They all howled.

Mr. Turnbull took up the story again. "Anyhow, there was some sort of scandal, and Mae divorced Mr. Creighton and hightailed it out of town with Herman. They wound up in Texas. The story goes that Herman's mother hunted them down and dragged poor Herman back to Belleville by the ear, an' that was the end of that." Mr. Turnbull punctuated the moment by spitting out a stream of chewing tobacco.

After the laughter died down, they went on to talk about
Nanny's father, F.C. Jones. "He practically owned this
town, including the sawmill and the cotton mill. His house
is right there yonder." He pointed to a lovely white clapboard
house at the end of the main road. "That house there, with
the brick. The brick's new, but that's the very house that F.C.
Jones built. Yep, Mae was raised with a silver spoon in her
mouth all right, but then F.C. lost everything in the crash."

F.C. Jones's house, where Nanny was born

No wonder Nanny never lost her bloodlust for money,
marrying time and time again hoping to land a gold mine.
Never happened.

When I told them that Nanny wound up having six
husbands—as far as we knew—and that when she died at

eighty-one she was dating a forty-year-old jazz musician from Redondo Beach, California, they didn't seem surprised.

Mr. Turnbull pulled me aside and asked me if I was related to "that gal on TV, Carol Burnett, 'cause I know Mae is related to her and some Meltons, too." I told him, yes, I'm her daughter. A few minutes later Duane joined us, saying, "Hey, did you know that the Meltons and the Joneses are related to Carol Burnett?" To which Mr. Turnbull replied, "Who's that?" and winked at me, never giving it away. I gave his arm a conspiratorial squeeze and bid them thanks and good-bye.

As it was Saturday the hall of records was closed, but the cemetery was right around the corner and "some of them Joneses and Meltons are buried there." So off I went.

It was a beautiful spot, and generations of local families are buried there. I paced up and down the rows of markers, some so old they were unreadable. A gravedigger was working on a new grave, so I didn't disturb him. I couldn't find a Melton or a Jones, so I got back in the car, prepared to head back out of town. The gravedigger waved at me, so I stopped and rolled down my window to say hello. "What are you doing here, young lady?" I told him I was looking for some family and mentioned their names. He said, "I know where they are, but it's not here. They're in another cemetery 'bout three miles up the road." I hesitated for a moment and he said, "Just follow me!" and jumped in his truck heading through town and up the most beautiful hill, surrounded by big land with homes set back off the road, cows, etc. The sun was about an hour away from setting, so the light was absolutely gorgeous, everything looking magical.

He took me to a cemetery at the top of a hill overlooking a valley and the hill we'd just crossed. He got out of his truck and introduced himself: Logan White. When I told him F.C. Jones was my great-great-grandfather, he turned me around and had me look out over that incredible view. "See that valley? Remember that hill we just went over? Well, that's called Jones Hill, named after F.C. He owned just about all this land between here and Belleville." I told him I wished that land was still in the family!

Logan had a great scratchy personality (comes with the job, I suppose) and we found Henry Melton's grave immediately. Henry had been the rich one, and I gathered that Nanny's "boy toy," Herman, may have been a bit of a ne'er-do-well, as Mr. Turnbull told me that when they were kids Herman gave him and his brother some homemade wine that he remembers to this day.

"That good?" I asked him.

"Nope. My head hurt so much the next day I couldn't put my hat on!"

We hunted around for Herman's grave to no avail. But F.C. Jones was there. Plain as day. Born 1854. Died 1933. Next to his grave was the headstone belonging to Hubert O. Jones, son of F.C. and Dora Jones, who died when he was fourteen, playing baseball. The baseball had hit him hard in the chest and he dropped dead on the spot. F.C. had run out to the field, picked up his son, and cried out to the crowd, "I'll give all my money to anyone who can bring him back!" His heart was broken. The inscription on Hubert's headstone read:

> Remember friends as you pass by
> As you are now, so once was I
> As I am now, so you shall be
> Prepare in life for eternity

Then Logan asked me if I was related to you, and when I told him yes, he said that his wife had written a letter to you years ago, talking about the family, and that you had written her back a real nice note. He told me about the Jones legacy, how the town folded in the crash along with F.C., how Mae is famous to this day, and on and on.

Mr. Turnbull encouraged me to retire to Belleville, but not to live there now when I'm so young. There's no money to be made there. But it's a nice town, he said. And I know that to be true. All the folks I talked to, including the mayor (Mayor Kenny) and his wife, Mary, were so open and free with information and stories, telling them like only southerners can, and especially Hill People.

As I left Belleville, I felt parts of myself were starting to make more sense. How I'm drawn to the hills and mountains, how hillbilly music speaks to me in a way that

is totally animal, how listening to revivalists (I'm talking foot
stompin', speaking in tongues, holy rollers) on the radio
(as I did most of the day today) has a deep-rooted sense
memory for me. Not sure if it's some genetic cell memory
or a past life thing, but I felt so up and excited and happy I
started to cry.

Mama, I'd really like to go back to Belleville one day.

After reading Carrie's e-mail about Arkansas, I decided to make
the trip there myself. I thought it would be great fun to bring
Jody and Erin plus my sister, Chris, with Carrie giving us the
"tour." I had never been there, and I remembered Nanny telling
me all about Belleville (but, of course, no mention of the "scandal"!) and I wanted to see it all for myself. I mentioned this idea
to Carrie and she was all for it. All we had to do was set a date for
the following year. . . .

From: Carrie
To: Mama
Sent: Jan. 11, 2001
Subject: Grants, New Mexico

After Belleville I feel like my trip is truly over. Seeing the
house in San Antonio, then meeting the guys in Belleville and
hearing all about F.C. and Nanny—anything else could only
be anticlimactic. I'm looking forward to our getting back to
work again on *Hollywood Arms* after I get back home. I really
love working with you, Mama. It's truly amazing that we can

write together "long distance" the way we do. My excitement about our play and working with Hal Prince is unbridled. I was thrilled when Hal said he couldn't tell which one of us wrote which scene. The fact that we have the same "voice" proves that this apple *didn't* fall too far from the tree!

And I enjoy the fact that I'm able to swing back and forth between "Sunrise" and our project without going into a nosedive. Sure keeps the ol' adrenaline pumping!

Although we've been working on *Hollywood Arms* for TWO YEARS(!) with pauses along the way, and are very much into the "structure and problem-solving" of a theatrical piece thanks to Hal's guidance, I never for a moment forget how fortunate I am to "see" Nanny, your mama, Louise, and your daddy, Jody, come to life. Mama, I'm not writing about them . . . I'm writing *them*!! Of course, it doesn't hurt to visualize your daddy, Jody, as an "inebriated Jimmy Stewart, and just as sweet" (your description of him).

Jimmy Stewart was to be a Kennedy Center honoree in December 1983, during the Reagan administration. I had the honor of being invited to be a part of the tribute to Jimmy, singing "You'd Be So Easy to Love" (a song he introduced in the movie *Born to Dance*). I took Carrie to Washington, D.C., with me for the weekend festivities, which included a dinner hosted by the secretary of state on Saturday night, to be followed by a show and dinner-dancing the next night, December 5, which would be Carrie's twentieth birthday.

The other honorees that year were Frank Sinatra, Katherine Dunham, Elia Kazan, and Virgil Thompson.

At the Sunday-night dinner, Carrie and I had the privilege of sitting at Jimmy's table. He had always been my favorite actor ever since I was a little kid, and here I was with my own "little kid," Carrie, enjoying my idol's company. Carrie was just as thrilled as I was because she had been raised on watching Jimmy in *It's a Wonderful Life* every Christmas, and loved him just as much as I did.

Carrie, Jimmy Stewart, and me at the Kennedy Center Honors
on Carrie's twentieth birthday in 1983

The fantastic Joe Williams was up on the bandstand swinging and singing with the Count Basie Orchestra. When Jimmy learned it was Carrie's birthday, he got up on the bandstand, had the orchestra strike up "Happy Birthday," and sang to Carrie with Joe Williams chiming in to make it an amazing duet. The entire crowd joined in after a few bars (including Frank Sinatra!).

Carrie and I were both dumbstruck, and when it was over she leaned into me and whispered, "Wow, Mama. So tell me what's up your sleeve for me next year, when I turn twenty-one?!"

Oklahoma and the Texas Panhandle are not the prettiest areas I've seen, but I knew I was getting close to New Mexico because of the dramatic change in terrain. I couldn't live there, but the land sure is spectacular and the sunset tonight was one of the most stunning I've seen in my life.

Grants seems like a very nice little town. I'm wrestling with the idea of calling for delivery. Road food is awful, and I'm malnourished beyond belief. If I have to eat one more Hostess Fruit Pie I think I'll die.

From: Carrie
To: Mama
Sent: Jan. 12, 2001
Subject: Gunnison, CO!!!

HOME, Mama, HOME! I made it back OK, but I'm pretty bone weary. Felt queasy the past couple of days. Guess my body is tired from the long drive back. But oh, it's so good to be here!

I'm happy to have my kitties pile on top of me, and I'm spinning my comforter in the dryer so it's nice and warm when I get in bed. Ahh! Life's little luxuries . . .

Guess what, Mama! I'm now declaring the year 2001 to be "The year of the grown-up!" At thirty-seven, I think it's about friggin' time! I'll always be a rock and roll girl, a recovering addict with a bird-of-paradise tattoo on my shoulder, but in spite of all that (!) I feel myself becoming more of a woman, no longer a girl. I was driving today thinking that I've been working at what I love (acting, singing, writing, directing) for eighteen years. I've built this cabin, been married, and divorced. I've had a life!

And that life was preparation for this next, second half. And when I look ahead to "Chapter Two" I wish to take all these things that I've learned and done and make something wonderful, lasting, beautiful, and kind from them.

I'm sending you the ending of SUNRISE, even though I have more scenes to write—more of Kate and the cowboy's journey *before* they reach Graceland. So what you have up to now is a half-finished story, with a beginning, middle, and end. I just have to add to the middle part.

I love you.

Your pooped little daughter

From: Mama
To: Carrie
Sent: Jan. 12, 2001

Hi Baby, got the final "Memphis" scene. Wow. I kind of suspected what was going on halfway through the story, but I wasn't sure. The ending is mighty touching, and might come as a surprise to some folks.

I'm looking forward to the scenes you have yet to write. Thank you for all the e-mails and "Sunrise" pages you sent while you were on the road. I'm saving every one of them!

I have to admit I'm more than thrilled you're back. I was a bit anxious when you took off in your Jeep all by your lonesome, so I'm grateful to be able to breathe a little easier knowing you're back home in your mountains, safe and sound.

I know you're not much of a phone person, and I don't want to disturb you in case you might be writing or resting or whatever, so I'll keep e-mailing you. Also, I wrote a few more scenes for our play, which I'll send to you for your input and any notes you might have before I send them on to Hal. This is such an exciting time for both of us, isn't it?

I'm not surprised you're pooped. You packed so much into your relatively short trip. It'll do you good to kick back and get lots of rest. Promise me you'll do that! Even though you've declared that you're now a grown-up, you're still my baby, y'know. That fact will never change.

All my love, Mama

Time passed and Carrie and I didn't e-mail so much, since she was frequently coming out to Los Angeles to pick up some television acting jobs. But she found herself tiring easily, so in July she was happy to get back to Colorado where she planned to spend the rest of the summer doing some writing, but also catching up on some rest. I had been concerned about her lack of energy, so I was happy she decided to cool it for a while, back in her cozy Colorado nest.

From: Carrie
To: Mama
Sent: July 15, 2001

Well, I still seem to be under the weather. Saw the local sawbones and he seems to think acid reflux may be the problem. I'm on meds and should start to feel better soon. However, I woke up at four-thirty a.m. with terrible gastric cramps that lasted until around six. After that, I was feeling much better, but I couldn't get back to sleep. So guess what?

I WROTE A SONG!

It's a country song, like a bluegrass waltz. It's called "Spring Lament" and I think it's quite simple and lovely. It came to me quickly. The lyrics are so simple, about a sad soul who lost his love in the springtime. It's mostly in the delivery (I'm teaching myself to play it on the guitar, picking one string at a time).

Here goes:

SPRING LAMENT

The snow's all but melted
But the grass is still brown
Somethin' 'bout springtime
Gets me down

The days are gettin' longer
But the sun's in a cloud
Somethin' 'bout springtime
Gets me down

I heard a girl laughing
When I was in town
Somethin' 'bout springtime
Gets me down

A bluejay there yonder
He's not makin' a sound
Somethin' 'bout springtime
Gets me down

I looked for you darlin'
But you weren't around
I looked for you darlin'
But you couldn't be found
Maybe it's just that I'm bound
To be sad
In the springtime

Each day gets warmer
But it's cold in the ground
Somethin' 'bout springtime
Gets me down

Each day gets warmer
But it's cold in the ground
Somethin' 'bout springtime
Gets me down

And that's it. I'd love to sing it for you sometime.

It's funny how much I want to sing these days. Jumping up onstage with this band and that makes sense to me because I've been living so much in my head, writing and directing. I need the exercise of singing/performing. Oh, if only I could be one of those people who feels complete doing one thing. But I need to stretch, to challenge myself, to constantly reach for things I've not been able to reach before.

Attention deficit?

OR just unclipped wings?

CAROL BURNETT

From: Mama
To: Carrie
Sent: July 16, 2001

Hi Baby,

Loved the song you wrote. I'll love it even more when I can
hear you sing it. Sweetheart, there's no reason on earth that
you can't "do it all." After all, isn't that what you've always
done?

Love, Mama

After she left Pepperdine, Carrie began to actively pursue her
acting and singing career. In 1985 she landed the continuing role
of Reggie Higgins in the TV version of the movie musical *Fame,*
about a group of students attending New York City's High School
of Performing Arts. In its way, the show was a precursor to *Glee.*
Reggie fit Carrie like a glove; a kind of kooky, bohemian girl who
was the first in her school to wear dark nail polish and experiment with pink highlights in her blond hair! (These were Carrie's
ideas for her character, not to mention the boas!)

I was invited to be a guest one week. The script was titled
"Reggie and Rose." The story line featured me as Rose, a caf-
eteria worker befriended by Reggie. As a finale, we wound up
performing the classic "We're a Couple of Swells" dressed like
hobos.

Carrie and me as Reggie and Rose in an episode of *Fame*

We had a ball, and it was the first of several times Carrie and I were to act together. We appeared in a TV movie, *Hostage*. We played a musical mother and daughter on an episode of *Carol & Company,* and again in an episode of *Touched by an Angel,* where Carrie wound up being voted by the crew as their favorite guest star of all nine seasons. Why? Aside from always being on time, knowing her lines, and hitting her marks, I think it was because she never went back to her trailer between takes, preferring to sit and joke with the crew while waiting for the next setup. She also made it a point to know each and every crew member by name. She never forgot a single one.

Carrie and me as mother and daughter in
an episode of *Touched by an Angel*

Earlier, in 1988, Carrie starred in what was to become a cult classic, *Tokyo Pop,* where she played an American singer who goes to Japan and gets involved with a Japanese singer and his band that makes it into the top ten on Tokyo's pop charts. She also wrote and sang the closing number that played during the end credits.

She received rave reviews for her performance, including this one by *Los Angeles Times* film critic Sheila Benson:

April 15, 1988

Loping through downtown Tokyo with her seven-league stride, her shades on her nose, her white-blond hair tucked up under a leopard pillbox, Carrie Hamilton stalks through *Tokyo Pop* and straight into our hearts.

When you leave the movie, all that stays clearly in focus is Hamilton. Even silhouetted against a Niagara of neon, she sucks in all the scene's energy, inadvertently, and probably even unconsciously. It's useless to try to concentrate on anyone else when Hamilton is up there, radiating away.

Carrie as Wendy in *Tokyo Pop*

Carrie was on her way. The phones kept ringing with new job offers. She even got a call from Marlon Brando, who had a project in mind. And what did she do? She turned them all down and decided to form her own band, Big Business, and to write and sing her own music in clubs.

To my surprise, I found myself turning into a stage mother, and begging her to reconsider. "Honey, opportunities like this won't keep knocking at your door forever!"

"No, Mama, I don't care about being a 'star.' I just want to concentrate on something else that I love for a while. I don't know, I guess I *do* want to do it all."

From: Carrie
To: Mama
Sent: July 19, 2001

Hi Mama,

I'm feeling so very much better today. Still in bed, though. My doc here is bad at calling back but a good doc, so all should be fine.

Woke up early again, and am excited to get back to "Sunrise." I thought of a couple more scenes to help fill out the middle part of the story as I was drifting off to sleep last night. I'll send you what I get as it comes.

I've been thinking about Kate's "memory" of her life. There's something about women's lives being cyclical and fragmented as opposed to men's lives, which seem to go like a straight shot. I think this is mostly true. Seems that our lives are like a patchwork quilt, and we weave together threads of ideas, loves, losses, dreams, notions, into the fabric that becomes our lives. Feels like I'm stitching together Kate's life here—at least that's what I hope I'm doing!

It's very cold this morning, but the sun woke me up shining through the windows and I thought why not stay put? I'm fine to sit up now at my desk, but I kind of like the decadence of the whole working from the bed thing!

From: Carrie

To: Mama

Sent: July 22, 2001

I did a bonehead thing today. I accidentally smacked myself in the face with the mudroom door, leaving a big upside-down V-shaped welt on my cheek, like some sort of gang-related ceremonial mark. I shall adorn it somehow tonight (maybe with surgical glue and a few sequins), cause a fuss in Gunnison, and next week, perhaps, everyone I see shall have big red sequined Vs on their cheeks. I think wearing one of my boas will cap the whole thing off!

From: Mama

To: Carrie

Sent: July 22, 2001

That's my girl!

From: Carrie

To: Mama

Sent: July 24, 2001

Hi Mama. Well, I saw sawbones again today, and now he thinks it might be something called giardia (some kind

of nasty parasite) that's laying me low, which might have
been caused by drinking bad water! (I'm going to change
the filters.) He put me on this very powerful antibiotic
(Flagyl) which is supposed to kill just about anything inside
of me, including Jimmy Hoffa, just in case he's hiding out
somewhere down there.

The good news is I had no fever last night. It was the first
night since Tuesday that I haven't soaked through the
sheets. I feel a lot better today, although I'm still gassy. I'm
eating, albeit small amounts, and it's not taking me as long
to choke down a meal, so all in all, I'm hopeful. I'll see how
it goes. I'm certainly not any worse than I was.

From: Carrie
To: Mama
Sent: July 26, 2001
Subject: How can you be lonely with a parasite, and other
burning questions.

I looked up *Giardia* on the 'net, and found a picture. Looks
like a friggin' party hat with a string coming out of the
top. They call it a "cystic" parasite. Cute, huh? Somehow,
with the name Giardia, I pictured a chubby Italian guy in
my stomach with a huge plate over his head waiting for
my meals to drop! I'm asymptomatic in some ways. I'm
constipated rather than having diarrhea, which most people
get, and fever is unusual, tho it can occur. Still have some

cramping and pain. Ate a whole bunch of spinach last night in hopes of Popeye-ing this bugger outta me!

From: Mama
To: Carrie
Sent: July 26, 2001

I'm glad you're feeling better, but my view is that you should have a battery of tests ANYWAY. Darling, I really think you should get a second opinion. Is there another doc in the vicinity? I know you don't want to get on a plane and come out to L.A. (where I wish you were at this time).

What about Boulder? It's a big city where there are bound to be specialists. I'll be more than happy to pay for your stay in a hotel, in a hospital, or whatever! You shouldn't fool around with this, even though you're feeling a little better. Why wait? Yes, it's a pain in the ass, but you should be looked at by someone in the city in a sophisticated facility. It may take a day or three out of your schedule, but aren't you worth it?

Love, Mama

From: Carrie
To: Mama
Sent: July 30, 2001

My morning thoughts:

I will, of course, take care of myself. But I honestly have
been feeling better. You know me, I'm not one to rush to
the doc when everything's working okay. I'm not good at
running around getting tested for what might be. But I have
decided to begin exercising again, and will build myself back
up slowly. This has taken me down quite a bit, so I have
nowhere to go but up, and in a way, I'll have a somewhat
clean slate. So I'm choosing to look at the whole sweaty
episode as a positive one. Onward and upward.

My dear neighbor, Leo, is coming by today to show me how
to change the water filters and to take a sample to get
tested. I'm sure it'll turn out fine. I probably just got the
aberration, "The Lone Giardia," if that, indeed, was what it
was. Whatever the case, Mama, I'm getting better and that's
all that counts for me right now. I'm even going out to dinner
tonight! Mind you, I'm not a fan of Chinese food and NEVER
go out for it in L.A. or NY, but HERE (!) there is a wonderful
restaurant (run by Tony from Thailand!) that for some reason
agrees with me. Go figure.

I intend on rereading my pages of "Sunrise" today, all these
pieces of the puzzle that I'm just putting together willy-nilly,
that I pray will add up to a LIFE. I guess that's what we do in
reality, too . . . no real, honest-to-God "master plan," just . . .
life.

A pal sent me a personality test (that the Dalai Lama
supposedly came up with) and my life priorities wound up
being, in order:

Family

Career

Money

Love

Family first! If I had to choose between that and Career I would choose Family. Luckily, the twain meet often. As for Money, I've obviously been very blessed in this life, and I figure I'll always have just enough and sometimes extra. The Love part? Well, it's just not a priority 'cause I *have* it in spades with my family and my closest friends. As far as love goes, I suppose I expect love to always be there, so it's not a "priority"; it just IS.

From: Carrie
To: Mama
Sent: July 31, 2001

Mama, I think you might be right. My friendly parasite (or whatever the hell it is) is back with a vengeance. Also, I coughed up a little blood for the first time. I called sawbones and he has yet to call me back. Much as I hate to leave my mountains, I know I must head out to L.A. to nail this sucker once and for all.

Thank God for my good neighbors, Ted and Vera. They'll look after my house and feed Pee Wee and the kitties while I'm gone, which I hope won't be long.

One good thing, though—I'll be able to see you and Jody and Erin.

Love you . . .

From: Carol
To: All of Carrie's friends
Sent: Sept. 7, 2001

Thanks so much for your letters and e-mails about Carrie, and for your love and prayers. She's nearing the halfway mark in her chemo and radiation, and in the midst of all this, a couple of weeks ago she found and moved into a new little house she's renting in Franklin Hills. She spent her first night there last night. She's still driving herself to the hospital for treatment.

Her attitude and energy have been amazing. She cheers up the rest of us.

She has named the tumor in her lung Yuckie Chuckie, and has created two Japanese-action-cartoon characters called Kimo and Radi, who exist for the sole purpose of zapping Chuckie. She looks upon the treatments as her heroes. She makes it a point to go out somewhere every day, even if it's only around the block. Just last Thursday, she and her sister Jody hit a nightclub to hear a friend sing. I don't know how long she can keep this up, but she's raring to go to the mall with me this week, to look for dishes and sheets.

Meantime, I feel so helpless (because I am). Aren't mommies supposed to kiss it and make it all better? I wish I could go through this for her. The doctors will wait a bit after her course of treatments is over, and then they plan to operate. The lung will probably have to go, but they said she has a fifty-fifty chance for a complete cure. She's young and determined.

Carrie told me she has reached a Zen-like state after having gone through the fear, the anger, and all the other crappy demons after the shock of the diagnosis. She even feels that this whole experience may be a "gift" of some kind. She says she's putting things into perspective—things that would have sent her up the wall in the past simply don't matter now. Keep the good thoughts coming. . . .

Love, Carol

From: Carrie
To: Mama
Sent: Sept. 8, 2001

I hated having to leave my cabin for the craziness in L.A., but I get that I have to be out here for treatments. Anyhow, this is a charming little furnished abode on a quiet cul de sac, not too far from the hospital, so it's not so bad.

Mama, I've started writing about this particular journey. I figure I might as well make the most of it! Here's a story about what happened yesterday. Hope you like it.

This man, Harold, in chemo wasn't looking so hot when I walked in, all chalky and breathing hard, and generally looking like he shouldn't be ambling around but should be in a hospital bed. When I checked in for my treatment today, Harold was becoming a bit code blue, you know, choking and all of that, and it was awful. I tried to bury myself in a *Time* magazine, but I kept hearing Harold (I couldn't see him from where I was sitting, but I could see his lovely worried-sick wife, who was trying to get someone to do something!). They had given him Dilaudid in order to sail through today high as a kite, so he was out of it, and I mean OUT OF IT. Now the nurse (think Louise Fletcher as Nurse Ratched in *One Flew Over the Cuckoo's Nest*) says, "HAROLD CAN YOU HEAR ME," and Harold says, "Yessssss," and the doctor who finally came down to see him said, "HAROLD ARE YOU IN PAIN?" And Harold said, "There isssss nooo such thinnng as paaaain."

I mean for chrissakes he's on friggin' Dilaudid! What a dumbass question. It made me happy this jerk-off wasn't MY doctor, 'cause even on Dilaudid, I would have jumped outta that La-Z-boy, tubes and all, and socked him clean across the jaw for asking such a stupid question, and billing me $350 bucks an hour for his "expertise."

Anyway, I felt so bad for Harold, and tried to hide my face more and more in that *Time* magazine, and then Nurse Ratched (in a cutesy, singsong, "Shirley Temple" voice) tells Harold, "OK HAROLD, WE'RE GONNA GO GET SOME NICE FRESH AIR . . . NOW, WON'T THAT BE NICE?" Which is a friggin' lie because they are going to wheel him to emergency and he'll probably be in the hospital until he dies, and AGAIN I thought, goddammit, I'd sock her, I swear I would. How dare anyone patronize someone like that?

Jesus, the indignity. It was the first time it dawned on me that sometimes these healthcare "professionals" look at people who are sick like they are sick AND retarded. They use baby talk, for cryin' out loud! We are NOT babies, we're just sick, and I'll tell you something, just because Harold was on Dilaudid didn't make him lose his facility for complex thought. He was simply somewhere else, and that dumbass doctor and Nurse Ratched didn't have a clue that he might've been that way because he was loaded to the tits on synthetic heroin.

Then Nurse Stella loses it and yells at the other nurses in a strained nasal tone (I swear she could have given Louise Fletcher a run for that Oscar she won). Meantime, I'm still trying to continue reading *Time,* really concentrating on an article about nuns and Alzheimer's research and this one nun who is 106 years old. She is still totally lucid, but her ninety-one-year-old nun pal isn't.

Anyway, getting back to Harold. I heard him say a couple of funny things. No one caught them except me. But I didn't laugh out loud, because Harold and I both know that it wasn't really funny. It was gallows humor to the nth degree, although even that becomes funny when you're staring at the hangman and he's got spinach in his teeth.

Anyhow, before the doc and Nurse Ratched wheeled him out, Harold said, "I'd like to thank my producers, my wife, and you, Doctor . . ."

I thought it was hilarious.

Okay, enough of that. I just had to get that whole episode out of my system. As far as now goes, I'm doing pretty well, treatment-wise. Hope I can be one of the lucky ones and not get too sick.

I brought my mirrored ball from home to lend to radiology, and also purchased some new CDs, since what they played over the speaker during "zap time" set my teeth rattling. Sucky choices, to be sure. Now we have Disco Fridays and the nurses and I get down and dirty (me in a boa, naturally) singing away, and I'll be darned if some of the younger docs don't wind up chiming in with us! Yep, we rock in radiology.

I've decided to shave my head before my hair completely falls out. "Proactive" is my motto. You know me, Mama, I can do wonders with scarves and hats!

The weeks went by (slowly), and Carrie finally finished her treatments: fifty-six minutes of radiation and seven chemotherapy sessions. It was October 2001. She wanted to go home to Colorado for a brief visit before she returned to California to determine if the doctors thought she might require surgery to remove part of her lung.

The doctors seemed upbeat about her response to the treatments and agreed that it would be beneficial for Carrie to get away for a short while. Carrie, Jody, Erin, and I were more hopeful than we had been in a long time.

It was at that time that I began thinking seriously about getting married again.

A few years earlier, I had met Brian Miller when I was appearing for six weeks in a musical in Long Beach. He was the contractor who hired the musicians and also played drums for this particular production. I admired his talent and his sense of humor. We became friends. After the show closed we went our separate ways. Brian moved on to continue his work as musical contractor for other venues in Los Angeles. Many months later, we ran into each other at an outdoor mall in Century City. We had lunch, saw a movie, and then had dinner together. After that we were pretty much inseparable. I introduced him to Carrie, Jody, and Erin, and they liked him immediately, which made me very happy. We planned to tie the knot in November.

Carrie was thrilled to be back in her cabin, surrounded by her beloved mountains. Having received loads of e-mails and cards from her friends and loved ones, Carrie was now able to take this time to send out her own "mass" e-mail response.

From: Carrie (in Colorado!)
Sent: Oct. 5, 2001

Hi there, gang!

As most of you know, I've been too busy to keep up with correspondence, and you have written asking WHAT IS GOING ON?!?!? So here's the update.

Lemme tell ya, having lung cancer sucks. The docs feel positive about my being able to beat it, since we went for the very, VERY aggressive treatments. I finished a little over two weeks ago. Not exactly how I'd planned to spend the second half of the summer! What's that quote? "Life is what happens when you're busy making plans . . ."

I feel empowered by God, my wonderful family, and my amazing friends (all of you!) who've helped me through the difficult times of treatment. I'm getting a little better every day, and again, being home is the best prescription ever. I've taken to unplugging the phone and leaving the answering machine off and just letting myself be quiet. It's an awesome and humbling thing.

I'm home now in Colorado for a respite from L.A. and a nice two-week period of quiet and country air. Can't get enough of it. If you want to know the truth about a well-worn cliché, home IS where the heart is.

I arrived in time for some beautiful fall foliage and unseasonably warm weather. It has just turned cold in the last few days, and we've gotten some frost and a teensy bit of snow. The deer are out and right now a doe and two yearlings are munching away on my lawn. . . .

The great news: Two weeks ago my tumor (Yuckie Chuckie) had already shrunk 75 percent. This, although not miraculous, is very unusual and wonderful news. Y.C. has gone from the size of a grapefruit to somewhere in between the size of a golf ball and a baseball. As the "real" shrinkage usually happens after treatment, there is still some significant shrinkage that can—and will, if I have anything to do with it—happen.

My oncologist and I were looking at the X-rays and talking about possibly saving the lower lobe of the lung. I return to L.A. at the end of next week for a round of tests, etc., to see exactly when (and if?) surgery will happen. At first they thought they might've had to take the whole lung out, so this is a terrific "maybe," which is swell. I sure do want to keep it!

I'm hoping to make the tumor DISAPPEAR altogether so I don't have to have ANY surgery . . . ya never know! ☺

Either way, the big sigh of relief was that all of the madness and discomfort of treatment was worth it. It works, along with a strong belief system, hypnosis, Chinese herbs, a circle of friends and family that continued to pray for me and put out wonderful, healing energy, acupuncture, and a myriad of other "alternative" treatments to support the Western medicine! Whatever the mix, I'm grateful as all get-out.

Aside from THAT, I will probably do another hootenanny the
first week of November if I can work it out with the band.
I can't wait to get back to singing and playing music. My
breathing is so much better. Just the fact that I can open my
mouth and make sounds come out is cause for celebration!

AND THAT is all the news that's fit to report. I can't thank
you enough for your e-mails and prayers. I know that all of
the good feelings out there have helped me to heal and
begin being a "survivor before the fact." I will keep in touch
as I can. These next two months may have me "down" for a
while, so please understand if you don't hear back from me
right away.

Trust me on this: I'm gonna be up and at 'em by the
beginning of next year. There's so much more to see and do.

Much love always.

XOXO, C

From: Mama
To: Carrie
Sent: Monday, Oct. 6, 2001

Hi Baby, thanks for calling. It was so good to hear your voice
sounding so strong! How terrific that you're sleeping, taking
walks, taking baths, and (omigod!) eating ELK!!! This is just

what the doctor(s) ordered. Okay, maybe the elk thing hadn't occurred to them, but I'm sure they'd approve.

Brian and I try not to watch too much of the news. It's so oppressive. Almost a month has gone by since 9-11, and all we can do is pray that Bush gets that sonofabitch, bin Laden.

It makes me so happy to know that you're there in your mountains, healing. I, too, wish you had a longer time to spend there. The important thing is that while you're there, you live in the present moment and not dwell on the clock or the calendar. Know that you are a huge chunk of my heart, and that I believe with all my soul you will be writing and directing and hootenanny-ing long after this trial becomes a dim memory.

I love you,

Mama

To: Mama
From: Carrie
Sent: Oct. 9, 2001

Thanks for all your encouragement, Mama. As for 9-11, I'm so glad I do not have a TV. I cannot wrap my head around it. It's just too horrible. I pray for the souls lost on that day and for their devastated loved ones.

In mid-October, Carrie returned to L.A. for her tests, and the doctors said the tumor hadn't gotten any smaller, which sent us all into a downward spiral. We still hoped that they might be able to shrink it some more in preparation for surgery. Carrie was able to spend some days at her little rental, but there were also days when she had to be readmitted to the hospital because of seizures.

Carrie was in and out of the hospital several times before it became evident that she would have to spend more time there.

She was admitted for the last time in November 2001. I remember tiptoeing into her room. She was asleep, and I sat on her bed and took her hand. She stirred and opened her eyes. She smiled.

"Hi, Mama."

"Hi, Baby." Looking around the room, I feebly joked, "So you couldn't wait to come back here again, huh?"

"I missed the food."

She sketched her heroes, Radi and Kimo, zapping Yuckie Chuckie (who resembled The Blob) with a ray gun, and taped her artwork on the wall of her hospital room so she could visualize the battle raging inside her. As the days went by, she would redraw this scene with Yuckie Chuckie getting smaller and smaller.

We were still working on *Hollywood Arms*. Carrie and I would kick around some thoughts for scenes to send to Hal Prince. I would take notes, type them out, and fax the new scenes to him in New York. It was the first time Carrie and I had worked in the same room. Until then I had been writing in Los Angeles and she had been writing in her Colorado cabin. And now, here we were, working together in her hospital room, with her in her bed, fighting this tumor. And in spite of it all, she was flush with fresh ideas for our project.

Brian and I were married November 21, 2001, with my girls' blessings.

On December 5 (Carrie's thirty-eighth birthday), I flew back east and attended casting auditions for *Hollywood Arms* with Hal. The brilliant Linda Lavin had already accepted the role of Nanny. Frank Wood was cast as Jody. Carrie had been in on these choices. She had loved all of Linda's work, and the two of us had seen Frank a couple of years before in his Tony-winning role in the Broadway production of *Side Man*.

We had both said, "That's our Jody!"

We had yet to find our Louise when the lovely Michele Pawk came in and read for us. The actors' union, Equity, allowed us to tape Michele so I could introduce the new Louise to Carrie. I flew back home and went immediately to the hospital to show Carrie the tape of Michele's audition. Carrie approved whole-heartedly.

She then gave me some wonderful news. "Mama! Guess what! I *won* the Women in Film award at the Latino Film Festival for my short movie *Lunchtime Thomas*!!!" She was the first non-Latino to ever win in that category. It was a very happy day. Jody picked up the award and presented it to Carrie a couple of days later, in her hospital room. Again, another happy day. We all visualized Yuckie Chuckie wasting away as Carrie happily polished off the large lunch on her plate, and kept it down!

By late December, Carrie was confined to her bed with an occasional outing in a wheelchair. The tumor in her lung had spread. She had developed some small tumors in her brain, which took away her ability to walk. Her spirits were still up, though, because there was the possibility of an operation to remove them. She was gung-ho and filled with hope. We all were.

The head nurse told me she had asked her one day how come she could smile so much, and Carrie had replied, "Every day I wake up and *decide:* 'Today I'm going to love my life.'"

"Mama, I want to give a party here in the room on New Year's Eve. You think the nursing staff would be okay with that?"

I checked with the head nurse at the desk and she said she'd be more than okay with it.

On New Year's Eve, Carrie gave a party in her room with her sisters and several friends in attendance. The fare was potluck, and balloons and confetti were the decorations. "Auld Lang Syne" was sung by all at the stroke of midnight, and nobody on the floor complained.

Several days later I was dealt a blow when the brain surgeon told me the operation wasn't going to take place. The tumors in Carrie's brain had spread. She would not be leaving the hospital.

Diary entry:
Jan. 3, 2002

> *Carrie doesn't know. I don't want her to know. She's still hoping the tumors will shrink. I* can't *lose my baby. Please no, please no, please NO! God, are you there?*

By mid-January, Carrie had grown very weak. I knew she knew what was happening when she handed me a piece of paper with these lyrics written on it.

Dance, dance for me
Dance with the stars
Laugh, laugh for me
Wherever you are

Sing, sing out loud
Like angels do
Remember me
The way I'll remember you

Love, love for me
With all your soul
Cry, cry for me
As I grow old

See, see me from the edge of Heaven's eye
Feel for me 'cause feelings never die

I'll remember you
My very special friend
Until we meet again

"Mama . . . forgive me?"

"For what, sweetheart?"

"Smoking."

I hugged her very hard.

"Mama . . . maybe you could finish "Sunrise in Memphis" for me?"

"Oh, honey, I'm not sure I could write what you were aiming for."

"It's okay. Mama?"

"Yes, baby?"

"Am I headed for Graceland?"

Carrie died the morning of January 20, 2002. Jody and Erin were with her. Brian and I drove to the hospital immediately. Toward the end she had suffered and endured so much. I remember holding her several times after she had been through a seizure. She'd look at me and cry, "Mama, this is just not acceptable!"

At the time, I was torn between wanting her to let go, yet wanting her to hang on. . . . (Was this a selfish wish on my part?)

Looking at her now, I saw peace on her beautiful face. She looked serene. I was relieved for my baby. She wasn't going to ever suffer again. Still, I couldn't stop thinking, "It's not supposed to happen this way. *I'm the one who should go first.*"

Diary entry:
Jan. 20, 2002

She's gone. Is there a worse pain? I don't think so.

I didn't want to get out of bed. The covers provided me with a kind of safety net. I would doze off and then wake up to the startling ugly truth of it all.

It was *Hollywood Arms* that saved my sanity. My husband, Brian, helped me enormously by pulling down the bedcovers and encouraging me to finish the play that Carrie and I had started. "You owe it to her." I knew he was right. I owed it to Carrie, and I owed it to Hal Prince. We were scheduled to premiere the play at the Goodman Theatre in Chicago in April 2002. I had to finish it all by myself, but I also had to believe that somehow Carrie would be there beside me.

Brian flew to Chicago with me to help me settle in, and set up my computer and printer in the hotel room. On the plane, I said a prayer to Carrie: "Baby, please be with me, I need you. Give me a sign." When we arrived, waiting for me in the suite was a beautiful array of flowers—birds-of-paradise! The card read, "Welcome to Chicago! See you tomorrow for our first rehearsal. Love, Hal." I called his room immediately.

"Hello?"

"Hi, Hal. We're here. Thank you so much for the flowers. How did you know they were Carrie's favorite?"

"I didn't. I just asked the florist to send over something exotic."

Carrie, Carrie, Carrie . . . are you really here?

The next night, after our first rehearsal, Brian, Hal, and I went out to dinner. The maitre d' brought over a complimentary bottle of champagne. He showed us the label. The name on it was LOUISE, Carrie's middle name, and my mother's first name. These two moments were enough to bolster my confidence. I honestly believe that they were the signs I had prayed for on the plane. I was able to write the new scenes that were required during this tryout period in Chicago. Hal was my support and Carrie was my inspiration. To top it off, it rained on opening night. Rain. Carrie's favorite weather and mine, too. Brian collected it in an empty water bottle and later transferred it to a sealed perfume bottle.

We were set to open on Broadway in the fall.

We buried Carrie's ashes in three places. A small cemetery in Los Angeles was the first, with only the family and a few close friends present. We placed a bird-of-paradise on the gravesite. A hummingbird with a pink head hovered above.

Carrie had told me about a special mountain she would often climb in Gunnison, where she would sit under her favorite tree and read. We flew to Colorado. Her neighbor told us where the mountain and tree were located, and the word got out that we would have a ceremony at two p.m. Practically the whole population of tiny Gunnison showed up.

We all arrived at the spot at the foot of the mountain at the same time and began the short climb to Carrie's spot. The whole group of us was about halfway there when suddenly it got dark and the heavens opened up. Everybody scurried back down the mountain and into their cars to wait for the storm to pass.

At the first sign of rain, my daughter Jody cried out, "Carrie's here!" I was elated. Carrie and I had always talked about how much we loved rain and here it was, for the first time in three months, in Gunnison, pelting down with a vengeance.

It began to clear up and once again we all climbed back up the mountain. There it was: Carrie's tree. A hole had been dug next to it for her ashes. Her beloved Great Dane, Pee Wee, had died and was cremated a few weeks before, so we had his ashes in a container that we would place next to Carrie's. We all stood in a circle. I passed the urn with her ashes around, and several people in the circle placed their hands on it as they spoke about the love they had for her and how she had "livened up things" in town on many occasions.

Vera and Ted were Carrie's neighbors. Vera spoke of their fond memories of Carrie:

She was loved by everyone she touched around here. Ted and I first met her when she and her husband were remodeling her cabin here at Sapinero. They had literally removed the roof when the rains came. They were going around the neighborhood asking for tarps. We became instant friends and Ted did a lot of work on the cabin.

At the time, Carol, we didn't know you were her mother. To us, she was just Carrie, a wonderful friend. She was like a daughter to us. Months later, we found out who she was, and asked her about it. She nodded, laughed, and hugged us.

One of our favorite memories is of the day when Carrie told Ted she wanted to write a screenplay in which he would play a part. He said, "I'd be happy to play your dad or your uncle." Carrie's response was, "Oh no! I want you to be my boyfriend." Ted loved that.

My memories of her are her big smile, her hugs, and her high-heeled boots. Also, you never knew what color her hair was going to be from day to day . . . even purple! She was so down-to-earth and just ordinary folk. She loved animals as much as we do. We took care of her critters many times.

After she got so sick, we had been keeping in contact with her sister Jody and knew the end was getting near. When we learned of her passing, it was so sad, but we were glad to know she wasn't suffering anymore.

Something strange happened. Carrie had given us a present of an answering machine and it went dead at the same time she passed away. Maybe it was a message from her, but the thing is, we still have the machine and it's working fine. She was so special to us.

We buried the containers in the ground, and Carrie's friends and neighbors covered them with flowers. Birds-of-paradise.

Brian and I drove back down the hill and decided to have

one last look at Carrie's beloved cabin. We had paid her a visit in her Gunnison digs a couple of years before. We had driven over from where we were vacationing in Telluride one morning, stopping on the way at an antique store, where I spotted an old Tiffany-style lamp that would appeal to Carrie's sense of décor. As we drove up the driveway to her home that first time, I was surprised at the vastness of her property, forty acres surrounded by majestic mountains. She and Pee Wee ran down the driveway to greet us. The two-story cabin was a little gem. The downstairs housed the living room, kitchen, and a dining room table. It was all open, with no walls dividing the space. The upstairs (which she had built with the help of neighbors) was entirely devoted to the bedroom and bath. The shingled roof had been hand-painted by Carrie—every single shingle! Outside on the porch was her rocking chair.

Visiting Carrie at her cabin in Colorado with
Great Dane Pee Wee in the background, 2000

I collected two things from the cabin to bring home: the Tiffany lamp, which she had loved, and one of her hand-painted shingles. Brian had once again collected the rain in a water bottle, which he later transferred to another sealed perfume bottle.

Presenting Carrie with the antique lamp

In June 2002, my sister, Chris, my nephew Max, and I flew to Little Rock, Arkansas, and drove through Russellville, arriving in Belleville two hours later. I had spoken to the mayor (Mayor Kenny) a few times by phone before and had arranged the date for our visit, so we were expected. Special arrangements had been made for us to rent a small house near a golf course just outside of town for our three-day visit, but unfortunately, Brian, Jody, and Erin weren't able to make the trip at that time.

After we unloaded our suitcases we hopped into the car and headed for Belleville, just a few short miles ahead. As we drove into town I was surprised and touched to see a sign reading, WEL-COME CAROL BURNETT AND FAMILY. Otherwise, it was exactly the way

Carrie had described it. One main street, one café (the Memory Lane), one post office, one main store, one gas station, one fire station, one courthouse, and Ruth's Beauty Parlor.

Mayor Kenny and his lovely wife, Mary, took us to the Memory Lane Café for dinner. The place was packed, and we were greeted by the locals with open arms. The dinner was down-home delicious.

The next day we met the same old geezers Carrie had met when she first hit town that Saturday afternoon (was it really only a little over a year and a half ago?). There they were, big as life, hanging out at the same old gas station. Mayor Kenny introduced me and they all said they remembered Carrie's visit. Amazing. It might have been Mr. Turnbull (the one who first recognized who Carrie was) who said to me, "Yep, that was some fine young lady. Never forget her. That smile of hers was wide as a barnyard door."

A smile as wide as a barnyard door

Logan White, the gravedigger, was equally enthusiastic about having taken Carrie to F.C.'s gravesite. "She was excited as all get-out over seeing where her ancestors had been laid to rest. She said that someday she'd like to come back and meet the whole town. Even said she'd get her hair fixed at Ruth's!"

We were taken over to F.C.'s house, where Nanny had been born. We were told that it had once been the finest house for miles around in these parts. It still looked pretty fine, with its new brick facade. The next day Mayor Kenny, who tooled around town on his motorcycle, handed me a helmet and I climbed up behind him and held on for dear life as we headed out to the cemetery. My sister and nephew followed us in the car. I had Carrie's ashes with me.

We reached Jones Hill, and found F.C. Jones's headstone. And now here I was, standing where Carrie had stood eighteen months ago. I took her ashes out of the container and scattered them over F.C.'s gravesite, then placed a bird-of-paradise on top, and as I was doing that, I heard Carrie's voice say to me, "Mama, I'd really like to go back to Belleville one day. . . ."

After Carrie died, I received many kind letters of condolence. Some of her friends wrote about their memories of times spent with her.

Dear Ms. Burnett,

My name is Kevan and I loved Carrie so very much. I thought I'd send you one of my favorite memories of her.

Carrie was such a wonderful friend to have and a wonderfully fun person to be around. I was forever asking to borrow clothes, shoes, or jewelry from her, she always obliged and fondly referred to me as the most voracious "prop queen" she had ever known! It wasn't long before the various parties we

*would attend or hold became unofficial competitions for us to
upstage each other, either in outfits or behavior. It was always
with much fun and love. I have to say Carrie outshone me every
single time!*

*I remember a party I held at my house where Carrie turned
up in the most outrageous Marie Antoinette costume complete
with powdered wig and two footmen (!) by her side just to help
her get her incredible dress through my front door. "We're here,
dahling," she announced, and promptly gave me the most elegant
curtsey one could ever receive.*

*The next day I called Carrie and said, "Once again girl, you
upstaged me on every level."*

*"Nonsense, Kevster," she replied . . . "Don't ever forget, I'm
just you without a penis!!!!!!!" She was INCREDIBLE. I miss
those days so much!*

Xxxxx, Kevan

Dear Ms. Burnett,

*Here is a very specific memory of one of the times I went to a
"Carrie Hamilton House Party." Carrie's parties were always
diverse, strange, and wonderfully weird, and that night was to be
no exception.*

*As I was driving to the Hollywood Hills with my wife,
Shawnda, for the latest event at Carrie's house, I had no idea
what was in store for me that night. Upon arriving, we said
our hellos to the usual cast of characters. Old, young, gay,
straight—all there for an evening of fun and laughs.*

Truth be told, I'm more of a wallflower, sticking by people

I know and with whom I can easily converse. However, as the party progressed, I found myself in the kitchen, with a group of people who were mostly strangers to me. I could use the saying "one thing led to another," but a cliché would not accurately describe what went down.

Unplanned. Unscripted. Unusual.

The subject of what Carrie would or would not wear was omnipresent at her parties. Standing with her and a small group of guys, that subject naturally came up.Without any hesitation or forethought, Carrie challenged us to see what it was like to "be her"!

I suddenly found myself in her bedroom with the guys as Carrie started passing out clothes and shoes. But the clothes were not for her or for us to merely look at, they were for us to wear! Very casually, nonchalantly, and with no qualms, our male clothing soon gave way to female clothing. But these weren't just any female clothes.These weren't just shirts and shoes one would see at any 'Insert Name Here' mall.

No, these were Carrie's clothes—unique, sexy, and damn hard for a guy to wear. Before long, I found myself walking down the stairs in a tight miniskirt and the highest high heels a man could possibly wear; all of us led triumphantly by Carrie.

That was Carrie. She made a non-drinking wallflower feel comfortable and at ease enough to put on a drag show in a room full of people. Something that I had never done and have never done since!

Thankfully, camera phones and social networking sites were not even on the radar at the time. All of us in that room have those unique and lasting visual memories, and that's more than enough. Thank you for the memories, Carrie.

Randy

From Philip Himberg
Artistic Director
Sundance Theatre Workshop:

July 8, 2002

Dear Carol,

The 2002 Theatre Lab starts today and I am enclosing our LAB BOOK, which is dedicated to Carrie.
    Her spirit is very much here.

Much love, Philip

Dear Friends,

The 2002 Sundance Theatre Lab is dedicated to the memory of one of our Lab alumni, Carrie Louise Hamilton, who passed away last January after a brave struggle with cancer. She was thirty-eight.

Carrie was a force: dynamic, funny, animated, and deeply passionate. As a writer, filmmaker, composer, singer, and actor, she exhibited a huge range of talent and craft. Seeing her play Maureen in the national tour of *Rent,* or Lucy Locket in *The*

Threepenny Opera, or seeing her award-winning film, *Lunchtime Thomas,* or on stage at an L.A. rock club, you knew you were in the presence of a true renaissance woman. And on her journey, Carrie accumulated an astounding array of collaborators, loving colleagues, and supporters. She believed in the power of friendship as much as she believed in the power of art.

In 1998, Carrie and her mother, Carol Burnett, applied to the Lab with a script they had adapted from Carol's memoir, *One More Time.* The play is a story of three generations of women and follows Carol's childhood years living near Hollywood Boulevard with her loving but alcoholic mother and her eccentric grandmother, who had migrated from Arkansas and Texas, when Carol was seven years old.

In her last year, Carrie had traveled to Arkansas and Texas to research the play, and perhaps as importantly, to connect personally with her heritage and the women of her family. I believe that the writing of *Hollywood Arms* was a very deep personal journey for Carrie: discovering from whence she came and from what stuff she was made.

In April, I attended the world premiere of *Hollywood Arms* directed by Hal Prince, at the Goodman Theatre in Chicago. It was, to be sure, a bittersweet opening. Death has continued to confound me. I ponder, "Where do people go?" As I sat in the Goodman auditorium, hearing words that flowed from the pen and heart of Carrie Hamilton, I got an inkling. Perhaps, as spirits of the theater, one of our most powerful legacies will be the written word and the interpretation of those words by artists and actors who are our collaborators.

Carrie Hamilton leaves many legacies through her art and her friendships. I miss her. It is with great pride that we at Sundance dedicate this 2002 Theatre Laboratory to Carrie Louise Hamilton. Carrie may not be here in person, but her spirit soars with us.

Philip Himberg

Jody and Erin wrote down a few memories of their own.

Mom, here are some memories I have of Carrie and me.
Love, Jody

Around 1999, Carrie called me one summer afternoon wanting to come down to my house in the Valley and visit for a while. I had some folks over and we were all hanging out at my pool, and I said I'd love it if she came. She was on her cell, and while *still* on the phone with me, she got in her car and started heading down from her place in Lake Hollywood to my house. She hummed "The Girl From Ipanema" as if playing a trumpet the *entire* way to my house (at least fifteen minutes), not hanging up until she arrived in my backyard!

This would not be the last time either. . . .

In 2001, Carrie had to be admitted to the hospital due to seizures and other complications from her cancer. This was her first admittance, and the first time she had been admitted to any hospital outside of rehab, so she was quite frightened.

Lonny and I had only been dating a little over a year. We came by the hospital to see how she was doing. The hospital had put a cot in her tiny room in case anyone wanted to stay with her. Carrie asked me to spend the night. Lonny had driven me to the hospital, so I was without a vehicle to get home the next day. Lonny offered to pick me up after he finished work the next day, so problem solved. He said his good nights and went home. I crawled into the little cot in the small hospital room to keep Carrie company. Then she asked me the darndest question.

"Lonny won't break up with you over this, will he?" she asked.

"Well, if he does, then I say adios," I replied.

"You sure?"

"Carrie, if he can't understand that I need to be here, then he'll never understand me for who I am."

She smiled and hugged me. I think that's when she really started to know how much she meant to me.

Erin wrote the following letter to Carrie:

When we were little, I would watch you all the time. Almost study you like a book. I idolized you. I wanted to be just like you in every way. You had a voice! And boy, did you know how to use it. You taught me how to play the piano. I was never very good at it, but I learned this one song (that I can still play today) after you took the time to teach me. You were a great teacher.

Throughout our too-short time together, you had always encouraged me to sing. What a gift! Thank you.

You were a seeker. You would seek out adventures, and people. You made so many friends. Everyone loved you. Everyone still does.

I remember when you were first sent off to rehab. I was around nine. I wanted to go with you. I thought if you left, you were going to die. Then you got sober, and you became a celebrity. The cover of *People* magazine. I think ours was one of the first families to go public with the struggles of addiction. You became an AA guru. To this day, I meet people who speak of your helping a lot of people who followed your courageous journey into sobriety.

That was who you were. You were always a very kind, reassuring, and positive person. I wish we'd had more time together. You were gone much of the time, and we lived in separate places for much of our lives spent sharing this Earth.

That lanky body and big toothy smile of yours. That's how I still see you, Carrie—beautiful.

And what I take with me is a feeling. A feeling of love and comfort—and gratitude that you were my big sister.

Jody, Carrie, and Erin: three (grown-up) peas in a pod

In late 2002, Brian and I were in New York. *Hollywood Arms* was opening at the end of October, and we were deep in rehearsals.

It felt good to be back working with Hal and our same cast. The show had been on hiatus since we closed in May in Chicago, and now here we were, about to be on Broadway. Again, I prayed that Carrie would be there with me.

One afternoon Brian and I took in a Broadway show and after the matinee was over we were out on the sidewalk hailing a cab, when a young man approached me.

"Excuse me, aren't you Carol Burnett?"

"Yes, I am." I waited for him to say something about the television show, which is usually what happens when someone comes up to me like that. Not this time.

"I was in the cast of *Rent* with Carrie in Boston."

"Omigod. How nice to meet you."

"I just want to tell you that Carrie saved my life. I was heavy into drugs at the time and had been in lots of rehabs that didn't take. I don't know how I made the shows, but I was able to perform and not get fired, even though I was using most of the time. Your daughter would come into the dressing room early for every performance, and sit and talk with me, telling me all about what she had gone through, and how she got clean. She didn't preach. I'd had it up to here with people, including my folks, preaching to me. With Carrie, it was different.

"I looked forward to those conversations night after night. I found myself wanting to be like her. I wanted her energy, her laughter, and her love of life to be a part of me. I quit the show and went into yet another rehab, only this time it was because I wanted to—nobody was pushing me. I've been clean for six years, and it was all because I wanted to be like Carrie. I just wanted to tell you that."

Later that week I received a message that a well-known psychic wanted to get in touch with me. I didn't know him but I knew of him, because he was pretty famous. He left his number. I called him and he said he wanted to give me a private reading. He told me he had dreamed that he was supposed to call "Carol," and thinking this meant his assistant, whose name was Carol, he rang her up. That led nowhere, and the next night the dream returned, this time with my last name. He didn't act on it until the dream persisted over several nights. He finally figured he was supposed to get in touch with me, so he called. He also asked me (if I accepted his offer) not to tell anyone that he would be doing this session without charging me. Of course I was intrigued. We made a date.

He showed up at my hotel room at the appointed hour on October 17. We sat on the couch and he asked if he could hold a piece of my jewelry. I gave him my ring. He was quiet for a few moments and then some images began to come to him. He said that Carrie had orchestrated this meeting.

"Why?"

"Because she wants you to know she's here and she's fine."

"How do I know she's here?" I had wanted to believe in Carrie's signs in the past, but I was more than a little skeptical of this. I wanted proof that only Carrie could provide.

He told me to take notes, which I did. Not all of the things he said rang a bell with me, but an astonishing number were spot on.

1. She had a pet she loved with the initial "P." (Pee Wee, whose ashes are buried with hers in Colorado.)

2. Her illness wasn't diagnosed at first.
3. She had three services. (Los Angeles, Colorado, and Arkansas.)
4. At thirty-six or thirty-seven she took deep stock of herself, and declared that she was entering a second phase in her life. A new beginning.

A fragment of one of Carrie's e-mails popped into my mind:

I feel myself becoming more of a woman, no longer a girl. I was driving today thinking that I've been working at what I love (acting, singing, writing, directing) for eighteen years. I've built this cabin, been married, and divorced. I've had a life!

And that life was preparation for this next, second half. And when I look ahead to "Chapter Two" I wish to take all these things that I've learned and done and make something wonderful, lasting, beautiful, and kind from them.

5. The *Hollywood Arms* set has been flip-flopped. (The first design had the Murphy bed stage left. It was now stage right.)
6. Carrie had two tattoos. (At first I could only think of the bird-of-paradise, and then I realized I'd forgotten the first one she got, years ago. It was a small one on her upper left arm . . . of her zodiac sign, Sagittarius.)
7. She thanks me for putting up with her different hairdos and colors.
8. There will be some negative press for *Hollywood Arms* but she wants me to ignore it. Enjoy what we accomplished

together. No matter what happens, this project was our
gift to each other.

9. Something (an object) related to Carrie will be onstage,
"hidden" in the set.

10. Mama, when you walk out onstage I'll be there with
you.

He handed my ring back and the reading was over. I thanked
him for getting in touch with me. I attempted to pay him, but
he would have none of it. Even though some of the things he
brought up during the session didn't make any sense at the
time, I couldn't help but be impressed by some of the bits of
information—things he couldn't possibly have known. However, I knew he was mistaken about my "walking out onstage,"
because I wasn't acting in our play. I would be in the audience,
and in the wings at the end, waiting to hug the actors after
their bows.

We opened October 31 at the Cort Theatre. I was in the
wings watching our wonderful cast taking their bows, when Linda
Lavin (Nanny) pulled me out onstage to take a bow with all of
them. *When you walk out onstage I'll be there with you.*

I was later told that our stage manager had "hidden" a small
snapshot of Carrie on the set behind the Murphy bed.

What to make of all this? I don't know. Nobody knows.
Lots of people would say it's just a coincidence. Could be, but
I remember one time hearing someone say, "A coincidence is
God's little miracle, in which he chooses to remain anonymous."
I choose to believe the latter, maybe because it makes me feel
better.

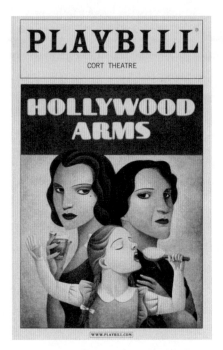

On Broadway

We received mixed reviews for *Hollywood Arms*. Some were pretty negative, and others ranged from mild praise to raves. Months later, I was thrilled when Michele Pawk walked away with a Tony Award for her performance as my mother, Louise.

The review I won't forget was written by *New York* magazine's John Simon (considered by many to be one of the theater's toughest critics):

Plays about passion are profuse and easy: heterosexual or homosexual, interracial or senescent, kinky or chaste. What is difficult and rare is a play about affection, which is what Carrie Hamilton and Carol Burnett's *Hollywood Arms* is. Authentic affection; not syrupy or sentimental, posturing or feel-goodish, gussied up for theatrical effect. *Hollywood Arms* is about real people.

He goes on to praise the actors and Hal Prince's marvelous direction. His review ends with this final paragraph:

If only this thoroughly endearing play and production could have been seen by Miss Burnett's daughter and coauthor, Carrie Hamilton, dead before even the Goodman Theatre premiere. One fervently hopes that the joy of such a true creation accompanied her on her final journey.

All I could think of was my baby and I had gone the distance.

I'd like to close Part One with one of my favorite e-mails from Carrie:

Mama, I've been thinking about that magician and endurance artist guy we saw in New York a couple of years ago (David Blaine, I think) who buried himself in a six-foot coffin inside a water tank for seven days, remember? Remember how everyone got in on the debate, *is it art?* I believed it was, indeed, as it brought out all kinds of emotions in the people who saw it (anger, fear, love, sadness, cynicism, etc.). My own fear was that people would walk away, and not think twice about what they saw (whether they liked it or not is barely relevant). Which brings me to the word *legacy.*

I think our legacy is really the lives we touch, the inspiration we give, altering someone's plan—if even for a moment—and getting them to think, rage, cry, laugh, argue, or walk around the block dazed. (I do that a lot after seeing powerful theater!)

More than anything, we are remembered for our smiles; the ones we share with our closest and dearest, and the ones we bestow on a total stranger who needs it *right then,* and God has put us there to deliver.

More later, Mama. . . .

What follows is Carrie's (half-finished) story "Sunrise in Memphis."

PART TWO

sunrise in Memphis

by Carrie Hamilton

The noise in the airplane cabin is terrible. Wind rushing at a terrific speed. Metal tearing, people screaming, objects crashing. The plane has a large rip in its side, and the scene is mayhem. People are being pulled to the hole by the force of suction, while luggage, food trays, and magazines fly through the air. It's a horrific scene out of our worst travel nightmares.

Incredibly, a girl in her early twenties is sleeping, oblivious to the mayhem around her. Kate, still dressed in last night's club clothes, her mascara smudged around her eyes, tosses and turns in her seat, unaffected by what's going on.

When her eyes finally do snap open, she takes in the scene with amazing calm.

"Oh, great, this is fucking great. I'm twenty-three years old and I'm going to die in a plane crash." Kate, not freaking out at all, is just observing. The noise is unbearable.

Elvis's "Blue Christmas" is playing somewhere, faint at first, but it gets louder and louder, until it becomes the only sound Kate hears . . .

On the single-lane desert highway, Kate is asleep in the passenger seat of an old but well-maintained pickup truck. She's wearing the same clothing and smeared makeup she wore on the plane. The wind is rushing by her open window, creating a sound not unlike what she heard on the plane. The radio is on, with Elvis singing away.

Kate's eyes open and she sees a man in the driver's seat, dressed in denim—work shirt, cowboy hat. He seems to be in his early thirties. He looks over and gives Kate a warm smile.

"Hey, do you feel like breakfast? You must be hungry."

Before Kate can absorb this, he has floated the pickup truck to an off-ramp and into the parking lot of a truck stop. Putting the truck in park, the cowboy gets out. Kate checks herself in the rearview mirror, picks up her tote bag, and ignores the cowboy, who is at her door, holding it open with a flourish.

"Ma'am?"

Kate shoots him a look and exits the truck. She strides ahead of him toward the diner. Somehow, he beats her to the door and holds it open.

"After you."

As Kate enters the café followed by the cowboy a waitress in her early fifties grabs a couple of menus and approaches them.

"Smoking or non?"

The cowboy answers, "Non," but Kate overrides him with, "Smoking."

The waitress gives the unlikely duo the once-over, hands them the menus, and shows them to a booth.

"Coffee?"

The cowboy begins to answer, thinks better of it, and looks to Kate who says, "With cream."

The cowboy smiles at the waitress. "Make that two."

As the waitress heads for the counter Kate digs around in her bag, finds her cigarettes, lights one, exhales, looks at the cowboy for a good long time, and finally says, "Who the hell are you?"

"Franklin Marshall Taylor, at your service. My friends call me F.M."

Kate inhales from her cigarette deeply, "How did I get here?"

"I drove you, Ma'am."

Kate scowls. "Look, I don't know who you are or what I'm doing here, but I'd sure appreciate it if you'd take me back to Hollywood. If not, I'll scream so loud it'll blast your balls off."

A moment later the waitress breaks the tension by bringing their coffee and setting it down. "What can I getcha?"

F.M. gestures to Kate. Keeping her eyes fixed on him, she answers, "Nothing. Coffee's fine."

"What about you, mister?"

"I'll have two eggs scrambled, white toast, two strips of bacon, and orange juice."

The waitress takes the menus and leaves. F.M. looks at Kate. "You should eat something. We have a long road ahead of us."

"*We* don't have anything, cowboy. *I* am going to the bathroom. When I return, I want you to have that truck of yours fired up and ready to head back to Hollywood. *Comprende?*" She abruptly gets up, taking her bag, and heads to the john.

She's washing her face at the sink with the pink granulated soap favored in truck stops when their waitress enters the bathroom and looks at Kate.

"Hey."

"Hi." Kate continues washing last night's makeup off her face.

The waitress gets out her compact, lipstick, and a teasing comb. "Rough night?"

"Apparently." Kate dumps her bag on the counter. Cigarettes, coins, matches, scraps of paper, a drawing pad, pencils, a small wallet, and a cell phone that is on but indicates no service. Its battery is very low. She begins gathering up the change.

The waitress smiles at Kate in the mirror. "Well, I think it's terrific."

"What's terrific?"

"Your trip!"

Kate looks at her, puzzled. "My trip?"

The waitress is looking in her compact, piling on the lipstick. "Yeah. You and the cowboy! I've always wanted to see Graceland. I saw Elvis in '72 in Vegas. He was just starting to get fat, you know, but boy, that man still packed a wallop! I was just a kid then, but I would've dropped everything if he'd given me the word. But, honey, that man of yours? Hoo-wee! Now *that's* what I call a hunk. Puts Brad Pitt to shame if you ask me. I'd hang on to that one if I was you. How long you two been together?" She turns around, but Kate is no longer there.

Kate looks around the restaurant. The booth where she and F.M. sat is now empty, the busboy clearing the remains of his half-eaten breakfast off the table. She looks out the window and sees him standing by the pickup truck. She marches out the front door and right past him to a phone booth.

Kate picks up the phone and inserts a handful of change. She listens as the phone rings and rings, until finally a tired-sounding male voice answers.

" 'Lo?"

"Jack, it's me!"

"Okay. I give up. Me who?"

"It's Kate. Asshole . . . it's Kate!"

"Jesus, Kate. It's nine in the morning. Call me back later."

"Jack, wait! I'm in trouble!"

"Are you in jail?"

"No. I'm in . . . to tell you the truth, I don't know *where* I am. I think I'm still in California. I got shit-faced last night at the Burgundy, and this morning I wake up in the fucking desert somewhere, in a pickup truck with some freakin' cowboy, my cell phone doesn't work, and he wants to take me to Graceland."

"Yeah. Okay. So what's the problem?"

"Well, you need to come get me!"

"Shit, Kate. It's practically the middle of the night, you don't know where you are, but you're with some guy, and you want *me* to come get you?"

"Dammit, Jack. I need your help. I'm not kidding."

"Oh, so *now* you need me? Little Miss 'I can take care of myself' wants me to drop everything to help her out?"

"Jack, please. I don't have time for this. Just write down this number, call me right back, and we'll figure out the best way to work this out. Please?"

"Why don't you have the Lone Ranger ride you back here on Silver?"

"I'm trying to tell you, I don't know this guy!"

"Well, you'll have plenty of time to get to know him on the wagon train to Memphis."

Then Kate hears a woman's voice, heavy with drowsiness, talking to Jack. "Who is it, honey?" Jack replies, "Nobody. Go back to sleep."

"Jack . . . ?"

"Later, Kate. This isn't a good time."

The line is dead. Kate bangs the phone down, then reaches into the slot for change. A nickel comes back. She bangs the receiver again, but no more money comes out. While she's frantically searching her bag for more change there's a tap on the door. It's F.M.

"What do you want?"

"You need more change?" He hands her several quarters. She looks at him, and he smiles. He *is* good-looking, and he's probably playing it for all he's worth. She grabs the change, pulls the door closed, loads up the phone, and dials. After four rings an answering machine comes on. Seventies porn music plays behind a woman's sultry voice. "This is Martine. I'm surfing porn sites so I can't come to the phone right now. I'm not in the mood to return calls, so don't bother leaving a message. Oh, yeah. Don't forget to have a nice day." *Beeep.*

The absurdity of both the message and Kate's situation is not lost on her. She bangs the phone down. "Shit! Shit! Shit!"

F.M. is back to waiting patiently by the pickup. Kate gathers up her things and exits the booth, approaching him. She leans up against the pickup truck and takes out a cigarette. She barely has it out of the pack before he produces a Zippo and lights it.

"No one home?"

Kate stares out at the desert. "No. No one."

"I can take you back if you want."

Kate studies him for a moment. "To what?"

"To your friends, your boyfriend, your family, your life."

Kate shakes her head.

"What?"

"All of it. The whole thing." She turns, pulls the passenger's door open, and gets in the truck. F.M. climbs into the driver's seat. Staring straight ahead, Kate announces, "Let's go."

"Where to?"

"Graceland, right?"

On Hollywood's busy Cahuenga Boulevard tires screech as a car slams to a halt. Kate yells at the driver who has almost hit her, kicking his bumper as he speeds away. She is with her friend Martine (from the answering machine), who's around Kate's age, also good-looking, hip, and very sexy. The girls are in their clubbing clothes. Kate is wearing her stomper boots and carrying a small backpack.

Kate yells after the car, "Pedestrians have the right of way, asshole!"

Martine laughs. "Tell that to the coroner."

The girls approach the Burgundy Room, a small, popular bar on Cahuenga. Outside, a black man sits in a rattan armchair. In his forties, wearing thick glasses, a sport jacket, tie, and a watch cap. Charles is the doorman and a sage to many of the Hollywood kids who frequent the Burgundy. Even sitting down, it's obvious Charles is very tall.

Charles smiles as the girls approach.

"Hey, Charles!"

"Martine. Kate. Hello there!"

"Has Jack shown up?" Kate asks.

"No. Not yet. How are you ladies tonight?"

"After having had a fight with my boyfriend and almost getting run over crossing the street, I'm just peachy. If I don't get a drink soon, I'm going to cry."

"Well, go on in and have a good time."

The Burgundy is dark and crowded. The loud music and din of the crowd is all-enveloping. Kate and Martine greet a few people as they work their way toward the bar. Yvette, the bartender, sees them and smiles as she serves another customer a drink, then comes over. Kate and Martine both lean over the bar and hug Yvette.

"Hey! I'm so glad you're here."

"Me, too," Kate says.

"Me, three," Martine adds distractedly, looking across the bar. "Who's *that*?" She has spotted a guy sitting alone who would be almost pretty if it weren't for the multiple piercings, tattoos, and what looks to be a very bad attitude.

"Not sure. He's new."

Kate follows her gaze. "Oh, puh-leeze. . . ."

Martine doesn't look back. "What? He's gorgeous."

"Yeah. If you like guys who eat glass for breakfast."

But Martine is already heading toward him. Over her shoulder she shouts, "That's perfect. Yvette, send me a Jack and Coke over there, and whatever he's drinking."

Kate shouts back, "How about the blood of freshly killed nuns?"

Martine flips her off and sidles up to the guy as Yvette says, "Haven't seen you for a while, Kate."

"Yeah, I've been working nights. I fucking hate it."

"Tell me about it. At least your customers aren't drunk guys with wandering hands."

"No. Much worse. They're OLD. 'Miss? These eggs . . . they're too runny, they're not runny enough, my nose is runny, could you blow it for me?' On a good day they smell like stale socks. God help me, I hope I never get that old. Would you pour me a margarita?"

"Double?"

Kate nods. "I just might get shit-faced tonight."

As Yvette goes to pour the drink Kate is grabbed from behind, lifted up, and kissed ferociously on the neck. It's Kenny, one of the regulars at the bar and a nighttime pal of Kate's. In his twenties, he's chubby, and wears glasses and a baseball cap that says FOG on it.

"Christ, Kenny! Put me down! I just ate!"

"Me, too!" He sets her down and Kate turns around and hugs him.

"I love your chubby tummy."

"Hey, I'm on a diet."

"You are?"

"Yep. I'm working my way down to obesity!"

Kate laughs.

The DJ puts on "Hot For Teacher" by Van Halen, which sends the bar into a tizzy. This is a Burgundy favorite. Everyone cheers and sings along. Yvette hands Kate her drink, which she gulps down before singing along with the crowd. The bar top gets doused with lighter fluid and set on fire. Everyone goes nuts. . . .

F.M. is driving through the dark on an empty desert highway. Kate's eyes are closed. They pop open suddenly, and coming out of her reverie, she looks over at F.M.

"Did I meet you last night?"

"You could say that."

"Did I fuck you?"

F.M. nearly loses his grip on the wheel. "No! No, ma'am . . . we didn't . . . not at all. I would never. . . . You'd had too much to drink."

Amused by his discomfort Kate says, "It's okay, cowboy. I believe you." Resting her head on the back of her seat she looks out the window at the starry sky and closes her eyes and drifts off again. . . .

As the night wears on at the Burgundy, people are dancing, making out, talking, drinking. Martine is in a lip-lock with the guy with the piercings, Kenny is singing along with the music, the burly male bartender has his shirt tied like a girl's around his "tits," and Yvette is pouring drinks like mad. Kate waits at the head of the line for the ladies' room. She bangs on the door.

"C'mon!"

Two girls emerge, rubbing their noses. Kate enters and a drunk guy tries to push in with her.

"What the fu—?"

"I was thinking maybe you and I—"

"I think you're gonna have to go fuck yourself, buddy, because I'm sure as hell not going to."

She pushes him out and locks the door. He pounds on it. Sitting on the toilet seat Kate pulls a plane ticket out of her backpack. She looks at it for a long time, her shoulders slumped. . . .

Kate is still snoozing when she hears her door open and feels someone gently shaking her. She rouses and looks at F.M. They're in the parking lot of a motel.

"I got us rooms here," F.M. says as he hands her a key. Number 5. Right in front of the truck. "I'll be next door in 4 if you need anything."

Kate gets out of the pickup carrying her tote bag, opens her room door, and flips on the light. F.M. is next to her at the door of his room, about to do the same. Kate stands in the doorway for a moment, staring into the room, not moving.

"You okay?"

"Yeah. Fine."

"Okay. Just let me know when you're ready to go in the morning." No answer from Kate, who's still standing there. "Good night."

" 'Night."

F.M. enters his room, shutting the door. Kate looks out at the parking lot, the pickup truck, the motel sign, the highway. She steps into her room, turns on the bedside lamp, and looks at the phone. She dials long distance and her own answering machine picks up. "Hey, it's Kate. Leave a message and if I don't call you back it's because I owe you money."

Kate punches in a few numbers and the machine tells her, "You have no messages." Kate hangs up. She sees herself in the mirror and leans her head back against the wall shared by F.M.'s room. She puts her ear against it, but hears nothing. Kate shuts off the lights. Neon leaking from under window shades shows her the way to bed. She crawls under the covers and falls right to sleep.

After a morning spent driving into the spectacular and endless desert sky, Kate and F.M. have parked on the side of the road. Kate sits on a rock eating a sandwich, and F.M. is perched nearby. She finishes her lunch in silence. Looking at him, she finally speaks. "I'm gonna need a toothbrush."

At the next truck stop Kate peruses the aisles. She's holding a toothbrush, deodorant, a pack of gum, and cigarettes. A trucker accidentally bumps into her when they both go to open the fridge.

"'Scuse me."

"No problem." He gestures for her to go first. She grabs a Coke and holds the door open. "Here you go."

"Thanks." He grabs a Coke, too. "Where you headed?"

"Memphis."

Smiling, the trucker asks, "Gonna see the House of Elvis?"

"Guess so."

"You're too young to remember Elvis."

"I've seen the videos."

"The videos, huh? What'd you think?"

"No wonder the girls screamed so loud. He was pretty hot-looking before he got fat."

The next morning when Kate steps outside her room a dilapidated, homemade RV, wood and drywall held together by baling wire, is parked next to F.M.'s truck. A man and woman in their mid-forties are tying things to the roof. Spray-painted on the sides are the words THE DEATH-WISH STUNT SHOW. The couple is dressed in secondhand splendor, not chic, but definitely individualistic.

As Kate rubs her eyes, taking in the scene, a mangy dog runs over to her, wagging its tail, and starts jumping on her.

The woman looks over and says, "Get down, Evel!"

"It's okay, I like dogs."

"Me, too. But this one has a bad habit of not paying attention to a word I say."

"It's 'cuz he's stupid," the man says over his shoulder.

Evel starts to ride Kate's leg.

"GET DOWN, EVEL!" This time the woman has caught Evel's attention. He stops.

"He's not stupid, Vernon, he's just got other things on his mind." She winks at Kate. "I'm Sylvia Halloran . . . an' this here's Vernon."

"I'm Kate."

"And you've already met Evel."

"Why do you call him Evil?"

"Knievel! You know. The famous daredevil."

"Ohhh. . . ."

"He's supposed to be part of the show, but I've never met a more scaredy-cat mutt in my whole life. Our last dog, Phoebe, why, she'd jump through a ring of fire or climb poles to get a toy. The crowds loved her."

"She was a good dog," Vernon says nodding.

"Yes, she was."

"What happened to her?"

"Just got old," Sylvia responds. "Bad hips. Couldn't jump anymore. Phoebe lives with my mother in a retirement village in Surprise, Arizona."

"Nice place," Vernon adds.

Sylvia makes a face. "If you like golf."

"There's nothin' wrong with golf."

"Shoot me in the head, Vern, I swear, if I ever decide I want to golf my life away."

Vern turns to Kate. "Y'know, you can drive the golf carts right down the main roads there!"

Sylvia laughs. "Malls, nothin' but malls, malls, malls. I hate it."

Vern smiles at Kate. This is obviously a well-worn argument. "Well, Phoebe sure likes it."

"Why wouldn't she? Mama cooks *steak* for her."

"Well, Sylvia, maybe I'll retire there with your mother and eat steak, too! But until then we've got some road to travel. C'mon, Evel!"

Evel jumps into his spot in the backseat.

Sylvia turns to Kate. "He complains, but the open road and show business is his life, just like it's mine. Well, Kate. Sure was nice to meet you."

"You, too."

Vern calls from the RV. "C'mon, Sylvia. We have to be in Deming by four o'clock!!"

Sylvia and Vernon fire up the vehicle, which coughs and spits.

Evel barks and they are off, leaving a cloud of light-blue smoke in the parking lot. Kate waves good-bye.

F.M. approaches with two coffees. "Sleep okay?"

"Not bad."

"Nice folks?"

"Yeah . . . real nice." Kate looks pensive.

"What?"

"Nothin'." Kate chuckles. "That's some kinda wonderful freaky relationship."

The speedometer on F.M.'s truck reads sixty-five miles per hour. As they cruise down the highway, they come upon the Death-Wish Stunt Show RV in the right lane. Sylvia and Vernon can't be going more than forty-five miles an hour.

As F.M. passes them he and Kate wave. Sylvia and Vernon stick their heads out of the windows waving, laughing, and honking away. Kate starts laughing, too. She looks back and laughs even harder. F.M. looks over at her and smiles. It's the first time he's seen Kate happy. It suits her.

Kate settles back in her seat, closing her eyes yet again. . . .

Outside the Burgundy a small line has formed, and Charles is checking IDs. Kate steps outside.

"Leaving already, Kate?" Charles asks.

"No . . . just need a break." She lights a cigarette as she leans against the wall.

After the last person in line enters the bar, Charles turns to Kate. "So, how's it goin'?"

"Okay, I guess. I don't know, Charles, I get so confused sometimes."

"What's so confusing?"

"Well, I'm supposed to go see my mom in Cleveland. Red-eye flight tonight. I haven't seen her since I was ten."

"That should be nice."

"Yeah, right. I thought so, too. Funny, I've been looking forward to this, but now I'm not so sure. I'm scared, I guess. I don't even know what she looks like now. And she sure as hell won't recognize me."

"I'm sure she'll be happy to see how you've turned out."

Kate shoots him a look. "That's a stretch."

"You'll probably be surprised at how much you have in common, even if you haven't been in touch. Family is like that."

Kate chuckles wryly. "Maybe that's what I'm afraid of. . . ."

The radio's turned up loud to compete with the road noise from the pickup truck's open windows, waking Kate from her reverie. She takes off her shoes and wriggles her toes. She looks at F.M. for a long while.

"Mind if I draw your picture?"

"Me?"

"See anybody else around here?"

She reaches back into her bag and grabs a pad of paper and a charcoal pencil. Opening the pad, she brushes the page three times with the back of her hand and begins making bold strokes. F.M. sits up straighter in the driver's seat.

Kate smiles at him. "Relax."

"Easy for you to say. You're not the one being stared at."

"F.M., do you ever take that hat off?"

"To shower, to sleep, and in church. That's it."

"You go to church?"

"Of course I do. Don't you?"

"Nope. Never been."

"Not even when you were a kid?"

"Nope."

"Wanna go with me on Sunday?"

"I hope you're kidding."

"It's fun."

"Fun? Church?"

"Afraid to find out?"

"Not me."

Everyone gathering outside the Baptist church is very dressed up. Kate, still in her now very wrinkled club clothes, feels awkward and out of place. F.M. is still wearing jeans, but his hat is off, his hair combed neatly, and he has a sport coat on. They are walking toward the entrance to the church.

Kate clutches at F.M.'s arm. "I don't think I can do this."

"Why not?"

"Look at me!"

"You look fine."

"What I look like is weird next to these people."

A black woman approaches, wearing a large hat, gloves, and a frilly dress—her Sunday best. She's smiling. "Hi there!"

"Hello." F.M. flashes his grin in response.

"Haven't seen you two around before."

"Just passin' through, ma'am."

"Name's Beulah. Beulah Tynant."

"Franklin Marshall Taylor, and this here's Kate."

"Well, hello there, Kate. Aren't you pretty as a picture."

Kate self-consciously smooths her dress.

"I sure am glad to see you both here. We got a lot to celebrate today! Now, you all go in and getcha a seat. I do believe it's going to be standing room only today, praise God! I'll see you inside!"

Kate turns to F.M. "I can't do this."

"Of course you can."

"Well, let me put it this way, cowboy, I don't *want* to." Kate holds her ground as F.M. gives her a good long look.

"Okay. I don't want to force you. Mind waiting for me?"

Kate looks around. "No, I guess not."

"I'll see you in a little bit, then. If you need me, you know where I am."

He enters the church. Kate stands outside, watching the last members of the congregation go into the building. After the large doors shut she sits on the steps. It's not long before she hears an electric organ and voices raised in song. The sound of the gospel music is exciting, even through the heavy church doors.

Kate sits and tries to resist, but her feet are tapping to the rhythm. She looks at the doors of the church. Before she knows it, she's slipping inside.

The church is packed with people. There's a huge choir, and even a band. People are standing and clapping, shaking tambourines and raising their hands in the air. Kate leans against the back wall of the church, letting the sound and the joy wash over her.

After the service, as people file out of the church, F.M. sees Kate standing against a large tree across the lawn. He walks over to her.

"You get bored out here, Kate?"

"No."

"Wanna get some breakfast?"

"Sure."

Beulah comes over. "Kate! I hope you enjoyed the sermon."

"It was nice."

Beulah hands her a new Bible. "Here. I want you to have this. A little memento of your visit to Caldwell Baptist."

Kate takes the Bible and stares at it.

"And next time, don't stand all the way in the back there like some lost little lamb, y'hear?"

Kate nods.

"Now, F.M., I want you to take good care of this young lady."

"Yes, ma'am, I will."

"All right, now. I best get on my way. You two travel safely, now, y'hear?" Beulah crosses the lawn and climbs into a bus that has I THINK MYSELF HAPPY REVIVAL CRUSADE emblazoned on its side.

F.M. turns to Kate. "Did you notice that she didn't care what you were wearing?"

Kate puts the Bible in her tote bag.

On the second story of a motel's walkway, Kate sits on the floor, pensively dangling her legs through the bars. F.M. approaches.

"Mind if I join you?"

Kate looks up and nods. He settles in.

After a comfortable silence Kate says, "You know, I've been golfing my whole life."

"You must be pretty darn good at it."

"No. Not the game. The idea."

"Ma'am?"

"Seems to me that golf is just one example of most people wanting to be part of the same group. To belong. It's about feeling safe, I guess, and it's pretty much one of those things that's expected of you when you reach a certain age."

"I don't care for those golf clothes much."

Kate continues as if he hadn't spoken. "I'm like that. I do what's expected of me. Like everybody else in my crowd."

F.M. shakes his head. "I don't see how you can say that, Kate. I think you really stand out."

"No, I don't. We're all trying so hard to be different, which is almost funny in itself, and we all have the same opinions. We even dress alike. It's like an antipopularity contest that we're all trying to win. To be the weirdest. Kinda sad, really."

Quietly, F.M. asks, "Then why do you do it?"

"I dunno. It's just what kids my age do."

"You're not a kid, Kate."

"Yeah . . . I still am. I pout like a kid, I expect things like a kid, I'm impatient as hell, and I haven't got the faintest idea what being a grown-up is like."

"It's the same. 'Cept you're not as surprised by your sameness. There's only so many ways to dress, and so many opinions to hold, Kate. That's not what makes you different."

"What does, then?"

"The way you eat a sandwich. You start on the outside and leave big chunks in the middle—the good bits. Then you go at those. You don't ever tie your shoes single, you always double-knot them. Before you draw, you run the outside of your hand along the paper three times, almost like you're cleaning it, or putting your scent on it. And I've noticed that when you sleep in the car, your ankles cross."

Kate looks at him for a long moment before gently saying, "I don't see how that makes me different."

"That's what makes you who you are. Those little things, the odd quirks and habits—that's the everyday stuff that makes up a life. That's what folks will remember about you. That's what would make a guy fall for you."

Kate starts to smile. "You're not getting sweet on me, F.M., are you?"

"No, ma'am. But I can sure see how someone could."

Kate looks out over the parking lot. She's touched by what F.M. has said. "You're so nice to me. I can't figure out why you're so goddamn nice to me."

He's not going to figure it out for her. He just sits there looking out over the motel parking lot and the night sky with her. In a few minutes he gets up and dusts off his pants. "I'll bring you coffee in the morning?"

"Sure."

"Okay. 'Night, then."

He turns to leave. Kate calls to him. "F.M.?"

"Yeah?"

"Thanks."

Kate and F.M. sit at an outdoor picnic table. F.M. is still eating. Kate's half-finished plate is pushed to the side and she is sketching. The place is hopping, music being pumped outside through tinny speakers, people gassing up, talking, playing cards. Most have come from church and are still dressed up, although neckties are loosened and fancy hats have been left in the car. A group of old black men sit at the table next to Kate and F.M. Joe, at least seventy, is telling a story.

"Mr. Pembroke, see, he hated black folk. But he liked my uncle, used to have Uncle Lowell take him into town all the time."

"Yep," another elderly man chimes in. "I remember seein' your Uncle Lowell with Mr. Pembroke. Always bowin' and scrapin', he was."

"Yep, he sure did," Joe allows. "That's the way it was back then. Well, Mr. Pembroke, he hated anything black, even his black mules. He had one white one, tho' by the name of Teddy. Remember him, Herbert? Mr. Pembroke even kept that mule separate from the others."

"I remember that mule . . . white as snow."

"Teddy had no sense at all and was mean as a snake, to boot. But when Mr. Pembroke come to town he always told Uncle Lowell he wanted Teddy to be pullin' the cart. Didn't even want to be seen bein' pulled by a black mule."

Herbert chuckles at the memory. "That was one baadd mule, all right."

Joe continues. "So one day, ole Teddy jus' decides to lie down in the middle of the road, with Mr. Pembroke in the cart and everything. Now, Uncle Lowell starts beggin' the mule, then he gets to kickin' him, 'C'mon, Teddy! C'mon, mule, stand up!' And do you know what Mr. Pembroke says?"

Herbert, playing the straight man, says, "No, what'd he say?"

"He says, 'Lowell, what color is that mule?' An' my uncle says, 'Why, suh, that mule is white, suh.' And Mr. Pembroke says, 'Now, how do you talk to that white mule?' And Uncle Lowell says, 'Please get up, MISTAH Teddy, *please* get up!'"

With that the whole table cracks up. Kate, who has been sketching Joe and Herbert, smiles over at F.M.

Henderson Swamp is eerily beautiful. Trunks and roots grow out of the opaque water, the whole scene in browns, grays, and blacks. The truck is parked on the shore of the bog as Kate sketches and F.M. looks at a map.

"Where are you from, F.M.?"

"Well, accordin' to my mama, heaven."

Kate doesn't look up from her sketch pad. "Must be nice, heaven."

F.M. looks at her deadpan, but his eyes sparkle.

The next day Kate is sitting on a park bench in Natchez, sketching, when F.M. comes up behind her and places a big gift-wrapped box on the bench.

"What's this?"

"Aren't you supposed to open presents to find out?"

Kate opens the box and there's a very pretty dress inside. Kate pulls it out ever so gently, like it's made of butterfly wings.

"Why?"

"Well . . . frankly . . . that outfit you've got on . . ."

"Not exactly low-key?"

"No, ma'am, but that's not my point exactly. Well, I thought if you had another dress, we could do some laundry."

"Are you saying I stink?"

"No! No, Kate. You don't—"

Kate sniffs her pits as an older woman walks by, looking at her disapprovingly, shaking her head. "Oh, man! I sure as hell do! Why didn't you say anything?"

"Well, it's not exactly the easiest subject to bring up."

Kate laughs. "How many days have I . . . ?"

"Since yesterday. Least that's when I noticed it."

"It's those little motel soaps. They don't lather up, and most times they just break into little pieces." Kate looks at the dress. "It's so . . . different. Not exactly what I'd usually wear."

"I hope it's the right size."

Kate spots a filling station down the road. She heads toward it, the dress over her arm. "Well, I'm gonna find out! Be right back!"

She hoofs it down the street while F.M. sits on the bench looking after her. She turns back for a moment. "F.M.!"

He smiles and waves. Kate takes a good, long whiff of her armpits again as a knot of tourists hurries past her. She looks at them and rolls her eyes dramatically. "Hey, it's not *that* bad!"

F.M. cracks up.

Kate is wearing the new dress that F.M. bought for her, with her stomper boots. She looks feminine, yet very much her own person. Spying a beautiful old clapboard house with a sign outside, PATRICIA'S KITCHEN, Kate turns to F.M. "Could we go there for dinner?"

"Absolutely."

Patricia's Kitchen is a very frilly southern home whose living room has been converted into a small restaurant. Filled with flowers, pictures of fuzzy animals, and lots of paintings and sculptures of Jesus and the Virgin Mary, the restaurant consists of only a handful of tables. There is one other couple dining.

A middle-aged woman approaches F.M. and Kate. She smiles briskly and says, "Welcome to Patricia's. I'm Patricia. Table for two?"

"Yes, ma'am." F.M. smiles as she ushers them to a table. "Would you care for a beverage?"

Kate says, "I'll have a glass of red wine."

"Oh dear, I'm sorry but we don't serve alcohol in this establishment. Gilby's across the way does, though. . . ."

"No, that's okay. Do you have cranberry juice?"

"That I can do."

Patricia looks toward F.M. for his order.

"Water's fine."

An hour later, as F.M. and Kate are finishing their meal, Patricia approaches the table. "Will that be all for you folks this evening?"

"Yes, ma'am." F.M. grins. "That was a great meal."

"Do you know someplace we could stay the night here in town?" Kate asks.

"Well, yes, as a matter of fact. You could stay right here! We run a small bed-and-breakfast. Only three rooms, but they're very nice."

Kate looks at F.M. who says, "Well, thank you, ma'am, we'd be honored to stay here."

"Very well. Ina May?"

A young woman who is clearly Patricia's daughter enters from the kitchen. Although she's the same age as Kate, she could be from another world. Conservatively dressed like her mother, she has the dowdy appearance of someone twice her age. Shyly wiping her hands on her apron she says, "Yes, Mama?"

"Would you show this nice couple to Room 2?"

F.M. and Kate quickly glance at each other and then both speak at the same time: "Oh, no! We'll need two rooms."

Patricia gives them a confused look, to which Kate reacts with a rueful grin. "He snores like a jackhammer. I haven't had a decent night's sleep in days."

F.M. doesn't miss a beat. "I'm sorry, honey. . . . I told you I'll see the doctor just as soon as we get back home."

"Well, I'm sorry to say we only have one room available. Mr. and Mrs. . . . ?"

"Taylor." Kate puts her arm around F.M. "It's okay. I can put up with the racket for another night. And it's such a nice place, isn't it, honey?"

F.M. nods, and Patricia says, "Ina May, show Mr. and Mrs. Taylor to their room. Do you have any luggage?"

"Nope!" Kate replies. "We'll just get whatever we need from the car."

Patricia watches F.M. and Kate follow Ina May up the stairs, noting Kate's boots. She fondles the cross around her neck.

As Ina May opens the door, the pink and red of the room is so overwhelming it nearly blinds Kate and F.M. Everything is overstuffed and flowery. Pictures of Jesus and Mary adorn the walls. The bed, however, looks like it might very well be made of clouds. And there's a huge clawfoot tub in the bathroom.

Ina May hands the room key to F.M. As she closes the door behind her she says, "Complimentary breakfast is served downstairs from six 'til nine."

Kate looks around the room, touching everything. Sitting on the downy bed, she spots the tub through the open bathroom door. "Oh, look at that!"

"Nice. . . . Why don't you take a bath?"

"You bet." Kate looks over at F.M. "Is this room okay with you? I know the color scheme leaves a bit to be desired."

"It's kinda like living inside a bottle of Pepto Bismol."

Laughing, Kate gets up and begins filling the tub. Half an hour later she's lolling happily in a bubble bath, talking through the door to F.M.

"I mean, Martine is one to talk. She picks the grossest guys, the meanest of the mean. Jack may not be a prize, but he was nice to me at first. I don't know what happened to him. Maybe the thrill was gone or something. . . . So tell me something about your love life, F.M." No response. "F.M.? Hey, are you there?"

Kate climbs out of the tub, wraps herself in a towel, and steps into the bedroom. F.M. is asleep on the floor bundled up in his coat, one of the pillows from the couch under his head. Kate looks at him for a moment. He's out like a light. She sits on the bed, staring at him, then takes the comforter off the bed and gently places it over him. Then she crawls into bed, looking at the moonlight coming in through the sheer pink curtains. F.M. begins to snore. Kate laughs quietly to herself, then grabs her sketch pad, wipes the paper three times with the back of her hand, and starts to draw.

The next morning Kate sits quietly sketching the flower beds in a lovely garden in back of the B&B. F.M. is inside, settling the bill with Patricia. Ina May exits the house, averting her eyes from Kate, but sneaking looks as she walks. She fills up a pail and moves to water the flowers.

"Will this bother you?"

Kate looks up. "No, not at all. It's Ina May, right?"

"Yeah. Stupid name, huh? It was my grandmother's."

"It's not stupid . . . it's old-fashioned."

"Like everything in my life. You have no idea how lucky you are. You're out there in the world. I love your clothes."

"But I got the dress right here in Natchez."

"It's the way you wear it. You're a woman of the world."

Kate laughs. "I'm only twenty-three! Hardly a woman of the world!"

"I'm twenty-three, too, but you'd never know it. I've never been out of Adams County. Mama thinks everything I need to learn is right here."

Kate looks thoughtfully at Ina May. "Well, lemme tell ya, it ain't that great out there."

"Well, I'd like to see for myself." Ina May lowers her voice. "You wouldn't by any chance have a cigarette on you, would you?"

"Sure." Kate hands her one, along with a matchbook.

After a furtive glance at the house, Ina May lights the cigarette. "Ever been to New York?"

"No."

"Well, that's where I'm gonna go. I wanna see the Rockettes and the Empire State Building and go to CBGB."

Kate laughs. "CBGB's."

"Same difference. I've read all about it. It's famous. Everybody all dressed up. Great music."

"I dunno. I remember hearing that it closed."

Ina May's face looks stubborn. "Well, there's lots of other places to see in New York City, although I don't know how I'm gonna get there. Mama never lets me go anywhere or do anything."

"But you're an adult," Kate says. "You can go anywhere you want."

"With what money?" Ina May sighs. "No—my life is all mapped out. Get married, have kids, spend a lifetime, and then die in this town, before I ever *really* lived. An' all the men in this town are jerks. I mean all of 'em."

"I hate to say it, but it's like that pretty much everywhere."

Ina May looks surprised. "Your husband seems real nice. Cute, too."

Kate shifts in her seat. "Yeah, that's true . . ."

Just then Patricia pushes open the back door. "Ina May? Could you help me in here? I want to move the couch in the dayroom so I can vacuum under it."

Ina May discreetly stubs out her cigarette. "Yes, Mama." The back door swings shut.

Kate slips the rest of her pack of cigarettes into Ina May's apron pocket, and gives her a conspiratorial look. Ina May smiles gratefully. "Have a good rest of your trip."

"Thank you. And good luck."

The back door opens again. "C'mon, Ina May. Those dust bunnies ain't gettin' any smaller." As Ina May passes her mother, Patricia lovingly moves a strand of hair out of Ina May's face. A sweet, motherly gesture that's not lost on Kate.

F.M. steps outside, too, then he and Kate wave good-bye, get in the truck, and drive off.

Kate and F.M. have pulled into yet another motel parking lot.

"Oh, Christ, not another dump." F.M. doesn't answer. "I'm sick of this. Do you hear me? I'm bored. Here we are again, at another crappy motel. You'll go to your crappy room, I'll go to mine. I'll pace around the room, open up the crappy little soap in its crappy little wrapper, try to get comfortable on a crappy mattress, turn on the TV, switch the channels every three seconds, and wish to hell I was someplace else."

F.M. tries to lighten up the moment. "Well, what do you want to do?"

Kate looks across the road at a bar. She gets out of the car. "I want to go over there."

"Kate!"

Kate waves good-bye to him as she walks toward the bar. F.M. watches her go.

An hour later, Kate has had a few and is playing pool with some hard-looking men. A band plays good-time-Charlie honky-tonk. Kate is one of the few women in the bar and definitely the prettiest. Kate leans suggestively over the pool table to reach a shot. Some of the men are watching her, while the other patrons are eating, drinking, dancing, and carrying on. Kate downs a cocktail, sinks her shot, and high-fives one of the guys playing pool.

A few minutes later she is spun out on the dance floor by one of the men she's been playing with, not entirely bad-looking but rough. Later still, the band is breaking down their equipment while the jukebox plays a slow song. Kate and her new friend are dancing, both very drunk. He begins kissing her neck and rubbing up against her. She responds to him, hungry for some physical affection. It's getting obvious that this is only going to go one way.

Kate and her dance partner stumble out of the bar as the lights are being turned off. Closing time. They have their arms around each other. Kate sees F.M., yet she saunters right by him with her new companion. F.M. calls to her.

"Kate!"

With her back to him, Kate flips him the bird. F.M. runs up to her, spinning her around. The man Kate is with slurs his speech. "Whoa there. . . ."

"Fuck off, F.M."

Her companion looks at F.M. "This your old man?"

"No."

"Then I'd 'preciate it if you'd getcher hands off the lady."

F.M. ignores him and tugs on Kate's arm. "C'mon, Kate. . . ."

Drunk and belligerent, Kate pulls away. "Leave me alone!"

"You heard the lady. Leave her—"

"This is none of your business," F.M. interrupts.

Kate shouts, "No. This is none of *your* business." Turning to her friend she says, "Now, Pete, where to?"

"My truck's right over there. . . ."

F.M. says, "Pete? Is that your name? I'm sorry to have to do this, buddy." And with that, he punches Pete so hard in the jaw that Pete drops to the pavement, out cold. F.M. rubs his knuckles.

Kate looks down at Pete, wheels on F.M., and smacks him in the side of the face with her bag, spilling the contents everywhere. "You asshole! You ruined everything. I was fine, you know."

"No, you're not fine. You're drunk."

"And that's just fine by me. I can handle myself."

F.M. watches her struggle to pick up her things.

"Yes . . . I can see that."

"It's *my* life!"

"You're right, Kate. It's your life." He pauses. "And what would you say about how it's going?"

F.M. turns away, getting into the pickup truck and driving to the motel across the street. Pete is stirring a bit, but Kate has lost interest in him. She sits on the packed dirt of the parking lot, a mess.

Some time passes before Kate wanders into the parking lot of the motel. F.M. approaches her and hands her a key. "Your room's right there."

Kate can't meet his gaze. She stands there for a minute. "I just wanted to have a little fun. How come you don't want to have fun with me, F.M.? Don't you think I'm pretty?"

"Sometimes I think you're so beautiful, I could cry."

Kate absorbs this. She looks up at him, teary. "Then why don't you want me?"

F.M. looks at her. She's pitiful, still a little drunk, and lovely. "I never said I didn't."

Kate turns toward her room. Putting the key in the lock, she turns one more time to F.M., holding his gaze. She then opens the door, steps inside, and closes the door behind her. F.M. stands there for a moment, then he enters his room and shuts the door.

Two teenagers approach Charles, outside the entrance to the Burgundy Room. Kyle, who looks about seventeen, has the hollow-eyed look of a teenager long on the street. His girlfriend, Lucy, maybe sixteen, also looks strung out—and about seven months pregnant. Kate stands against the wall, smoking.

"Hey, Charles."

"Hey, Kyle. Hello, Lucy. How's the little one doing?"

"Oh, she kicks all the time now. My ribs are sore."

Charles cocks his head. "She?"

Kyle says, "We think it's a she—"

"I hope she's a she. I want to name her Wendy," Lucy says, interrupting him.

"That's a lovely name."

"Hey, Charles. Look! I got my boots fixed. Remember they had a hole in the toe?"

"An' then the heels wore out," Lucy adds.

"It was a bad scene, man. I was walkin' all lopsided. And these are special boots. Can't just get a new pair like these."

"They're nice boots," Charles says, agreeably.

Lucy approaches Kate and bums a cigarette, joining her against the wall a few feet from Charles and Kyle.

"Dammit, Lucy. Why're you smoking?"

"It's just one. I'm stressed."

Kyle looks at Charles. "She gets down about the baby sometimes."

Charles nods.

"So anyhow, that dude on Hollywood and Wilcox? The shoe repair guy? He tells me he'll fix my boots if I sweep out his shop for a few nights. Easy trade for fixed boots."

"Yes," Charles agrees.

"No, really, man. These are, you know, special boots. My mom gave me these boots for Christmas. I hadn't spoken to her in about two and a half years. We had some problems. But then she tracked me down a couple weeks before Christmas. I mean, right out of the blue!"

Kate takes this in. Kyle continues. "And she says, 'Hey, Kyle, what do you need?'"

"You could've said a car!"

"No way, Lucy. My mom's not rich or nothin'. I couldn't ask her for a car."

"She bought your brother a car."

"Yeah. But he's not a fuckup. Anyway, Charles, I asked her for boots. And sure enough, they came about a week after Christmas. They were late, but they got here. New boots. Just shy of a hundred bucks. I had to work 'em pretty good, the leather was stiff. She even got my size right." Kyle looks at his boots. "That was two years ago." Kate takes the plane ticket out of her bag and looks at it for a long moment. . . .

It's late at night. F.M. is driving. Kate's asleep in the passenger's seat. It's raining out, the wipers barely making the road visible. The truck radio plays softly. The DJ's voice comes on:

That was Reba McEntire. News and weather is next. Rain all night, ladies and gentlemen. So, bundle up with your sweetie and enjoy Mother Nature's show. By late tomorrow it'll be sunny and hot, and you'll wish it was rainin' again. As for the news, investigators in Ohio have recovered the black box from the site of yesterday's—

The truck dies, the radio goes dead. Right in the middle of the road. F.M. tries to start the engine again. No good. Kate wakes up. "What is it?"

"Not sure." F.M. looks in the rearview mirror. "We should get her out of the road."

Kate has the window down, steering the pickup as F.M. pushes from behind. The rain is whipping hard and they're both getting soaked. After finally managing to safely park the pickup on the side of the road, F.M. and Kate settle in for the night. He's in the front, covered in jackets. She's in the back, with a blanket and her jacket as a pillow. The rain pelts the roof of the car.

"I'm really sorry, Kate. Guess I wasn't payin' attention to the gas gauge."

"It's okay."

"Are you cold?"

"A little, but I'm fine, F.M. Really. I've always loved the sound of rain on metal. The louder the better."

"Why's that?"

"I dunno. I guess it forces you to just listen. And wait."

They are both quiet for a few moments, before Kate adds, "I think when it rains like this, it's the only time in my life when all I do is just sit and breathe."

The truck falls silent again.

Kate wakes up the next morning. Groggy, she sees a note taped to the steering wheel. "Went to get gas and food. Back soon."

She stirs, puts on her jacket, gets out of the pickup, and stretches. A tidy but ramshackle home sits across the road, partly obscured by trees. Smoke rises out of the chimney. Kate takes it in before settling back into the car.

It's damp, cloudy, and cold. Bundled up in her jacket, Kate takes out her pad, wipes it three times, and begins sketching the house across the way. When she's finally finished with her sketch, she sits there, shivering. Not much to do now but wait.

An hour later Kate gets out of the car, crosses the road, and walks hesitantly up the path to the house. She doesn't get far before a woman's voice startles her. "Can I help you?"

"Oh, I'm sorry, I didn't see you."

An elderly woman, clearly blind, with one leg amputated below the knee, moves out of the trees, deftly using her cane for support. "Well, I didn't see you, either! But then again, I don't see much of anything these days. You the one with the broke-down car?"

"Yes."

"Mmmm. I heard it chug-chugging last night. Run outta gas?"

"Yep."

The old lady clucks to herself. "You kids, always in a hurry, but not doin' much plannin' for how to get there. You hungry?"

"Yes, a little. But I don't mean to impose on you."

"Nonsense, I'm glad for the company." Reaching out her hand, the elderly lady says, "I'm Emma Dee."

"Kate."

They shake hands and walk toward the house.

Inside it's clean, spare, homespun. Kate looks around at photos and bric-a-brac collected over the course of a lifetime, while Emma Dee is tending to some biscuits, eggs, bacon, and coffee on the wood-burning stove. A photo of a much younger Emma Dee, with a man and two little boys, catches Kate's eye.

Over her shoulder Emma Dee says, "That's my husband, Robert, and my kids. The tall one's Robert Junior, and the baby is Todd. That was taken back in 1965."

Kate is a little taken aback that Emma Dee could tell what photo she was looking at. "Where's your husband?"

"Oh, he's dead. Since '83."

"I'm sorry."

"Me, too. Robert and I met when we were two years old. Our mothers were best friends. Never was any doubt that Robert and I would marry. It was fate. God's will."

"You must miss him."

"Every day. I can't see the pictures too good anymore, but in my mind I can see him, young and runnin' around, laughing and playing catch with the boys in the yard."

"Where are they? The boys."

"Oh, they're gone, too. Not dead, but moved away. Country living doesn't offer much to young men with stars in their eyes. Robert Junior is in Chicago. Works for a big-time lawyer. Got a wife and three kids of his own now. They come visit 'bout once a year, but the kids get bored here. Think there's nothin' to do. I can't travel too well these days. Diabetes."

"Is that how you lost your leg?"

"Yes, ma'am, an' my vision, too. All happened within a year. Scared me somethin' awful, bein' alone out here, but I have my angel. Watches out for me."

"Your angel?"

"John." Emma Dee sets the breakfast down on the table. They settle in. "He come by here one day, askin' if I needed help."

"Why?"

"He's an angel, I'm tellin' you. At first I was suspicious, too, but he never asks me for anything. Won't even let me pay him. Just come by 'bout twice a week. Brings me groceries, helps cut firewood, tidies up, you know, things like that."

"A Good Samaritan?"

"I s'pose so. I've asked him, 'Why you do this for me, John?' But he just says it's his pleasure, then he's on his way. How's your biscuit, hon? Done enough?"

"Delicious. Best I ever ate."

A few hours later Kate looks out the front window, where F.M.'s truck can be seen across the street.

"It's quite a ways to town, Kate. I'm sure he's fine."

"Oh, me, too."

"You love this man, don't you?"

Kate laughs. "Well, it's hard to describe."

"Love usually is."

"I just feel safe with him. Totally safe."

"Ah. Sometimes we'd be in bed and Robert would shake me and say, 'Breathe, Emma! Inhale! You haven't taken a breath in so long you're gonna faint!' But y'know what, Kate? Truth is, when I was in Robert's arms I didn't feel like I needed to take another breath ever again. It was like he was my air."

Tears well up in Kate's eyes.

"What is it, child?"

"Nothing. May I use your bathroom?"

"Of course. First door on the right."

Kate walks down the short hallway to the bathroom, closing the door behind her. Catching sight of herself in the mirror, she turns away, lowers the lid on the toilet, and sits. Burying her head in her hands, she weeps.

Above the sound of the Big Mama Thornton record playing in the living room, Kate hears a knock at the front door and Emma Dee's voice.

"John? Is that you? Well, come on in!"

The front door slams shut, followed by the sound of footsteps and more greetings. Kate rises, splashing cold water on her face, hearing the muffled conversation through the bathroom door.

"Roses? It's not my birthday."

"Doesn't have to be your birthday for me to bring you roses."

Emma Dee laughs delightedly. "You are spoiling an old woman! I've got fresh biscuits, just out of the oven."

"No thank you, ma'am. I have to get goin' pretty quickly today. Let me just put these groceries away for you. Do you need any more wood for the stove?"

"No, I'm fine for a while."

Kate opens the bathroom door and makes her way back down the hallway toward the living room. "Emma, I should get going."

"Kate! I want you to meet John. John! I have a visitor I'd like you to meet."

John enters the living room. Kate stands frozen, staring at him.

It's F.M.

"Kate, this is John, the young man I was telling you about. John, this is Kate. She and her friend ran out of gas across the road."

F.M. says, "I saw the car," but before he can finish Emma Dee turns to Kate.

"We've had a lovely visit, haven't we, Kate?"

"Yes, we have. I really should go now."

"Well, your young man should be back soon."

Kate looks hard at F.M. "I'm sure he'll be here any minute." She bends over and gives Emma Dee a hug, breathing in deeply. "Thank you, Emma."

Emma Dee whispers, "You fly, child, but never lose sight of the ground."

Kate straightens up. "Nice to meet you . . . John."

"Nice to meet you, too."

Kate quickly walks down the path. Her emotions are a confusing jumble of shock, fear, and anger. Making her way to the truck, she quickly grabs her backpack, stands by the side of the road, and sticks out her thumb. A car passes.

F.M. comes running down the road toward her. "Kate!"

She starts walking at a fast clip, but F.M. catches up to her.

"Kate, please. Give me a chance to explain."

Kate's eyes focus on the road ahead. She won't look at him. "No."

"Please don't do this. It's dangerous to hitchhike alone."

Kate continues walking. F.M. stays where he is, watching her go. A truck approaches, and Kate sticks out her thumb. The truck stops, Kate jumps in, and leaves F.M. standing alone on the side of the road.

Inside the cab of the big semi, Kate holds her backpack and pocketbook in her lap. The trucker, a cowboy type about forty, shifts gears and looks over at Kate. She says, "Thanks for picking me up." He nods and turns up the country music on the radio. Kate looks out the window and watches the road go by.

Dusk is coming on when the big rig pulls into a truck stop. Kate hops down from the cab and thanks the driver, who waves and pulls away. Inside the truck stop everyone looks tired and dusty. Kate enters the ladies' room. Next to the sink she dumps the contents of her backpack and pocketbook. Not much there. A little change, some makeup, the dead cell phone, her club clothes, toothbrush, Bible, and sketchbook.

Opening the sketchbook, she begins turning the pages. The drawings are from Henderson Swamp, a motel sign, the church where Beulah gave her the Bible. She picks up the Bible, smiles, and puts it back in her bag. Returning to the sketchbook she comes upon a drawing of F.M. She stares at it, tracing her fingers across his face.

Back in the truck stop, Kate approaches the register with a can of Coke. After she pays for it, the clerk hands over her change and then reaches under the counter, producing a small bouquet of daisies.

"What's this?"

"You're Kate, right?"

"Yeah. . . ."

"Gentleman in the restaurant said to give these to you."

Kate walks over to the Truck Stop Café and Bar. F.M. sits alone at a booth, facing the door. As Kate enters, their eyes lock. She moves toward the booth, and slides in next to F.M. Keeping her eyes straight ahead, she speaks matter-of-factly, without a trace of self-pity.

"You know, my whole life I've been lied to, cheated on, and abandoned. No one has ever really cared for me. My own mother abandoned me, my so-called friends don't answer their phones, and any man I've ever trusted has turned out to be just another jerk. Until you. You seemed different. You seemed to really care about me. You seemed to want me to be . . . beautiful. And not for you, but for me. I was just starting to accept that, to not question it, and then at Emma's I find you lying to either her or me. And everything just fell apart. I felt more alone than I ever felt in my life."

F.M. remains silent. Kate looks at him. "It's just that when I met you it was like someone took a shroud off me, allowed me to see and feel and think for the first time. It's weird, but since we've been on this, what, journey, I've found myself letting go of what I was, what I didn't like about me, that for some dumb reason I kept hanging on to because it was all I knew. And now I don't need it anymore. I don't need to be with anyone who sucks the oxygen out of me, ever again."

F.M. smiles at her.

"I don't think you're a jerk, F.M. I'm not sure what you are, but I do know that I want to keep going with you. I'm not done with this trip. Am I?"

F.M. shakes his head. "No, ma'am."

"I'm not going to ask you about Emma, or about 'John,' about any of it. I've come to the conclusion that you must have your reasons, and it's just not for me to understand."

F.M. says nothing.

"Okay. This might be the craziest, stupidest boneheaded move of all time. But I trust you, F.M. I do."

There's a long yet comfortable silence between them. Then F.M. flashes a broad grin at Kate and pats her on the hand.

"What?"

"Nothin'. I just realized you haven't been smoking lately."

Kate puts her hand over F.M.'s as they sit at the booth, side by side.

Kate exits the Burgundy Room. Charles is sitting in his chair enjoying a slice of pizza. Martine and the tattooed guy she picked up in the bar saunter down the street, arms around each other. Charles follows Kate's gaze, and then holds out his slice of pizza.

"Wanna bite?"

"No thanks. I seem to have lost my appetite. Anyhow, my cab should be here soon."

Kate leans against the wall next to Charles. "You must see a lot of shit sitting out here, Charles."

Charles laughs. "That I do."

"Do you have a wife or girlfriend?"

"No, Kate. I lost my love seven years ago."

"What happened?"

"She died. Heart attack."

"I'm sorry. . . ."

"Started as the happiest day of my life. That morning I woke up knowing this was the day I would ask her to marry me. I couldn't wait until dinner, so at breakfast I got down on one knee and asked for her hand. We cried, we were both so happy. I was teaching full-time then. Evelyn worked for the phone company and was in night school getting her masters in sociology. She went to take a shower, and fell over in the shower. And she was gone, just like that."

"Oh, Charles."

"I wanted to die myself. Almost did, of sorrow, you know."

They share a silence. "My family pulled me out of it. I had locked myself in my apartment and wouldn't come out. I just knew I'd never have another love like that. And I really didn't want to teach anymore. Reminded me of Evelyn way too much."

"So that's why you're here?"

"For a while I was just wandering the streets a lot, singing at night on the corner."

"I remember. That's when you and I first met. I love your voice, Charles."

Charles smiles. "So the owner here offered me a job, since I already knew a lot of the kids in Hollywood."

"Don't you ever get bored out here?"

"No. I've got my books, and you kids have been like an extended family, especially you, Kate."

"We love you, Charles." Kate gives him a hug. Her cab pulls up and Kate gets in . . .

Kate has exited her room from a generic-looking motel across the street from Graceland, distinguished only by a huge mural of Elvis on the wall. Just as Elvis's "Blue Christmas" became the soundtrack for Kate's transition from the crippled jetliner to F.M.'s truck, now Charles's lovely baritone voice can be heard singing a cappella.

> Goin' home, goin' home,
> I'm goin' home.
> It's not far, jus' close by
> Through an open door. . . .

Over the years the wall surrounding Graceland has been richly inscribed with standard-fare graffiti. JIMMY LOVES SALLY, ELVIS LIVES, etc. Kate walks along the wall, running her hand along the bricks, as Charles's voice continues to be heard.

> *Work all done, care laid by*
> *Never fear no more.*
> *I'm jus' goin' home. . . .*

Kate sits in the back of a taxi, her head resting on the window glass. It begins to rain.

> *No more fear, no more pain*
> *No more stumblin' by the way. . . .*

Charles closes the iron gate at the entrance to the bar, and walks down Cahuenga Boulevard. A few people are getting in their cars, folks are making out, police cruise by. It's the end of a long night.

> *No more longing for the day*
> *Gonna run no more.*

Outside Graceland Kate stands at the gates looking at the building. A gardener on a ride-on lawn mower trims the grass.

> *Mornin' star lights the way. . . .*

Kate exits the cab at LAX. Working her way through the crowd at the airport entrance, she enters the terminal.

Charles stands on the street corner singing. Kyle and Lucy stand nearby, listening.

Restless dreams all gone. . . .

F.M. joins Kate at the gates. The way they look at each other speaks volumes. Charles's soulful singing fills the air like a spectacular sunset.

Shadows gone, break of day,
Real life has begun. . . .

F.M. takes Kate's hand. "Are you ready, Kate?"
    "Ready as I'll ever be."

An airplane soars, climbing steeply from its LAX runway. Charles's voice anoints the moment.

Goin' home, goin' home
I am goin' home. . . .

Street sweepers clean up the boulevard as Charles continues to sing.

Shadows gone, break of day. . . .

F.M. and Kate walk up the driveway of the property as the gates of Graceland slowly open on their own. The two step through the gates and as they do so, their images slowly begin to disappear.

Real life has begun. . . .

The TV newscaster's voice can't be heard, but a helicopter hovers over the scene of a plane crash, pieces of fuselage scattered over the terrain. The helicopter's camera pans in closer and closer to the crash.

Charles walks alone down the street. His singing can still be heard.

Shadows gone, break of day
Real life has begun. . . .

The news camera closes in on detritus from the crash. A backpack that has burst open. Kate's drawings flutter in the wind.

At Graceland the gates are closing. No one is visible. Not the gardener or his lawn mower, not Kate, not F.M.

The final notes of Charles's song ring out:

I'm jus' goin' home.

ACKNOWLEDGMENTS

My thanks to:

My agent, Phyllis Wender, who first encouraged me and kept the faith.

My editor, Peter Guzzardi, who lovingly guided me through this whole process with his expertise.

My Simon & Schuster editor, Trish Todd, who was behind this project all the way, and is the one who made it happen.

My husband, Brian, who was and is always there for me.

CARRIE HAMILTON
CREDITS

The role for which Carrie Hamilton first began to receive national attention was Reggie in the television series *Fame*. Guest-starring roles on other series soon followed, including: *Murder, She Wrote*; *Equal Justice*; *Beverly Hills 90210*; *thirtysomething*; *Walker, Texas Ranger*; *Touched by an Angel*; *Brooklyn South*; and *The X-Files*.

She also starred in numerous movies for television: *Love Lives On*; *Hostage*; *Single Women, Married Men*; and *A Mother's Justice*. Feature film credits include: Ralph Bakshi's *Cool World*; *Shag*; *Just Desserts; P.1*; and the cult classic *Tokyo Pop*.

She wrote and directed *Lunchtime Thomas,* which won the Women in Film Award at the 2001 Latino Film Festival.

Her theater career included acclaimed starring roles as Maureen in the first national touring company of *Rent* and Lucy in the Los Angeles Reprise production of *The Threepenny Opera*. She conceived the idea of writing a play based on her mother's (Carol Burnett) memoir, *One More Time*. Together they wrote *Hollywood Arms,* directed by Hal Prince, which premiered at

Chicago's Goodman Theatre in 2002 and went on to Broadway.

The prestigious Pasadena Playhouse in California named its balcony theater "The Carrie Hamilton Theatre" in 2005.

In 2009, Anaheim University in Tokyo established a Carrie Hamilton Scholarship Fund in her honor as a result of her performance in the motion picture *Tokyo Pop*.

PHOTO CREDITS

ABOUT THE AUTHOR

CAROL BURNETT is widely recognized by the public and her peers for her work on stage and screen, most notably *The Carol Burnett Show*. Named in 2007 by *Time* magazine as one of the "100 Best Television Shows of All Time," *The Carol Burnett Show* ran for eleven years, averaged thirty million viewers per week, and received twenty-five Emmy Awards, making it one of the most honored shows in television history. But it is Carol's artistic brilliance, her respect for and appreciation of her fans as well as her graciousness, integrity, warmth, and humor on- and offscreen that have made her one of the most beloved performers in entertainment and one of the most admired women in America.

As a highly acclaimed actress known for her comedic and dramatic roles on television, film, and Broadway, Carol has been honored with twelve People's Choice Awards, more than any other actress in the award show's history; eight Golden Globes; six Emmy Awards; the Horatio Alger Award; the Peabody Award; and the Ace Award. She has received the Presidential Medal of Freedom, is a Kennedy Center honoree, and has been inducted into the Television Hall of Fame. Carol has penned two *New York Times* best sellers, *This Time Together: Laughter and Reflection* and her memoir, *One More Time*.